Jack

Jack Russell Dog Owners Manual

Jack Russell dogs care, grooming, training, feeding and health.

by

Harry Hunstanton

Published by: IMB Publishing

Table of Contents

Acknowledgment

Thank you for taking a look at this valuable book on how to take care of a Jack Russell Terrier. This book will help you learn everything that you have ever wanted to know about how to handle such a beautiful and intelligent dog.

I know that the concept of having a dog in the home can be enjoyable but I also feel that you need to be prepared. I feel that this book will help you understand what you need to explore when it comes to taking care of a dog like this. This guide will give you the answers that you need.

I would like to thank my brother for helping me with writing this book. I would especially like to thank Belle, his wonderful Jack, for being a good example for this book.

The Jack Russell Terrier Club of America and the Jack Russell Terrier Club of Great Britain were both great organizations that helped me tremendously with regards to giving me information on some aspects of the dog breed. I actually learned more about the breed than what I already knew about before I got in touch with them.

Of course, the organizations are filled with people who have taken care of Jacks for generations. If you ever have additional questions about the breed that weren't answered here then you should contact one of these organizations to give you some useful answers.

Most of all, I would like to thank Charley and Star, my wonderful Jack Russell Terriers, for teaching me a few lessons about patience, responsibility and care. I am thankful for these two as they have been with me for all these years and have helped me learn all about how to be the best dog owner possible.

I hope that this guide will help you learn from my experiences with the Jack Russell Terrier. Trust me when I say that this is one amazing dog breed to have in your life.

Chapter 1: Introduction

Are you looking for a smaller dog that is not only handsome but also intelligent and loyal? If so, then you should take a look at the Jack Russell Terrier.

The Jack Russell Terrier is one of the most impressive dog breeds in the world. This is a dog that is known to be relatively small in size and to have plenty of appealing markings.

It is especially a dog that is great to have around in your life. If you are looking for a good companion who will be there with you for a long time then the Jack Russell Terrier may be the best option for you to consider.

This is a dog breed that has been around for quite some time and is also rather active. The dog has evolved and has become a popular working dog in many places as well.

This is a breed that you will learn more about as this book goes along. In fact, this book will help you learn everything that you have ever wanted to know about how to take care of one of these magnificent dogs. You'll learn about not only how to acquire such a dog but also the many key physical features that the dog holds.

You'll learn about how take care of the dog's diet, how to handle, exercise it and even how the dog will behave in various circumstances. You can also learn about the grooming aspects of this brilliant dog.

Details on the cost to own a dog like this will also be discussed in this guide. It does cost money to take care of it but you may find that the cost will not be as strong as what it might be when compared with much larger dogs that eat more and take longer to groom.

Everything that you have ever wanted to know about taking care of the Jack Russell Terrier is included in this guide. But did you know that having such a dog in your life can actually be better for you than what you might have ever imagined?

1) Health Benefits of Dogs

Having a dog around with you is great, but did you know that your health could actually benefit from having a dog in your life?

If you have a dog then you'll certainly feel much better with regards to your life. This is especially the case when you have a dog that is as active and energetic as the Jack Russell Terrier.

With this in mind, let's take a look at a few of the biggest health benefits that will come along with owning a dog. These benefits could be useful for any kind of pet but they will especially be true when it comes to the Jack Russell Terrier. Here are a few of the most popular benefits to explore with regards to the dog breed and your personal health.

You Can Get More Exercise

A great aspect of having a Jack Russell Terrier is that you will be able to get plenty of exercise. This comes thanks to how you can get your dog to go out on a walk or do other things that involve moving around.

This is a good advantage in that you'll have plenty of time to actively move and get your body to feel great. You will want to go from place to place and stay upbeat with regards to your dog and how it is behaving.

Remember, being physically active is important no matter what type of physical activity you're getting into. You have to be active so it will be a whole lot easier for your body to stay healthy. If you aren't active and you don't move around then it will be a whole lot easier for various health problems to develop.

Of course, you should still be prepared. The Jack is a very active and excitable dog that will certainly give you a fine workout.

They Are Great For Rehabilitative Purposes

Perhaps you have seen stories of people in rehab who have their own dogs with them. That's because a dog can encourage a person to become mobile, to interact with other people and to be more social. This can help anyone to get over physical problems and anxiety-related issues.

A good dog can encourage anyone to be social and can be a good link between people of all sorts. Having a dog as loyal and pretty as a Jack can make a big difference in your life.

Dogs Can Actually Detect Cancer

This is a rather unusual concept but a dog like a Jack Russell Terrier can actually detect unusual things in your body. Your dog might constantly sniff at something like a mole or other mark on your body that could be a sign of cancer.

You might be amazed at some of the stories you've heard about dogs being able to identify cancerous things or other problems within the human body. They can even identify these things as they start developing. This is important, as it is much easier for serious medical problems to be treated if they are spotted as soon as possible.

It is believed that this will be due to volatile compounds in your body changing in tone and potentially having scents that are significantly different from what is on the rest of your body. Either way, this is one of the more surprising things that you might get out of dog ownership. Think of a Jack as your lifeline in a case like this.

They Can Also Detect Low Blood Sugar

A 2000 report in the British Medical Journal found that dogs can experience behavioral changes when their caretakers have lower blood sugar levels. This is especially the case when it comes to diabetic people who have such dogs.

It's believed that the change in the owner's scent and the small muscle tremors that can take place within the body are recognized by dogs. The dog will see these as a serious alarm and will think that you are in serious trouble for any reason.

This is an advantage that is clear for those who have diabetes. However, pretty much anyone could develop low blood sugar for many reasons. Sometimes it might be because you haven't been eating a healthy diet or you actually haven't even eaten a single thing at all. If you do develop this issue then your dog will tell you by nudging you and encouraging you to possibly eat.

2) Never Leave a Dog Alone With Children

As great as it can be to have a dog in your life, you have to be very careful with regards to how the dog is to be treated. Specifically, you need to make sure you always keep your dog safe.

Children might like to play with dogs but it is important that you never leave your Jack Russell Terrier with children while no other adults are in a spot. There are many reasons why you need to be aware of this.

Children Might Be Too Rough

Sometimes a child can be tough and hard on a dog. A child might bother the dog too much or be very hard on it from a physical standpoint. Either way, it is important to be aware of how a child can go around such a dog and physically harm it.

Sometimes a child might pull on the dog's coat too much. The child may also pet the dog wrong. In some cases there might be times when the child pulls on the dog's tail.

These problems can especially get worse as the dog ages. The dog's body may not be capable of handling all that pressure as well as it used to. In addition, a smaller dog like a Jack will become more vulnerable to injuries that might be a result of the all that rough play.

The harm that might be caused will not be on purpose. Still, it is a real threat to consider. This is especially important for the Jack Russell Terrier, what with this breed being small.

The Injury Risk Is There

The Jack Russell Terrier is a good dog that is active and happy. It is not going to willingly attack a child. However, the dog might be too excited to the point where it could inadvertently hurt a child from all that motion and excitement. Again, the dog is not going to willingly hurt the child but it could potentially do this as a means of defending itself.

Don't Forget Cleaning

A child might not be fully aware of how to take care of a dog or how to clean after it. It's best to let someone who knows how to take care of such a dog stick around with it while that dog is around children. This is to at least make it easier for the dog to be treated the right way.

If you are going to have children around the dog then you should teach them about how to take care of such a dog.

With all these points in mind, we should start talking in detail about the Jack Russell Terrier. It is a truly amazing dog that deserves to be discussed in a little more detail.

Chapter 2: The Jack Russell Terrier Dog

What is it about the Jack Russell Terrier that makes it such a special dog? Let's start by taking a look at the history of this impressive breed to get a better idea of what it is that makes the dog so noteworthy.

1) History and Origin

The Jack Russell Terrier is a popular breed that has officially been around since around the late part of the nineteenth century. The breed was first developed by John Russell, a man from the United Kingdom who in the early part of the nineteenth century was interested in the field of sport fox hunting.

Russell was interested in Fox Terriers, the dogs that were often used around the UK for fox hunting. These dogs would get foxes to come out of their dens so they could be hunted down. The Fox Terrier is a dog that has been around in the United Kingdom for a long time. In fact, Romans who were in England right before the start of the Common Era actually noticed this breed. In short, the Jack has its origins from several centuries off in the past.

In 1819, Russell bought Trump, a Fox Terrier who had a fine build. The one thing that he wanted to do was to develop a terrier breed that was not only willing to do all that work to get foxes out of their dens but could also have plenty of energy to help with moving around large fields for extended amounts of time. In addition, the dog was supposed to be one that would not cause any physical harm to the foxes or have a taste for their blood. This was to ensure that there would be no sense of extreme fear between either side.

He also wanted to establish a new coloring pattern for the breed. He felt that the white coat and the dark tan spots around Trump's body made her the best possible template for preparing a new breed with a distinguishable style of its own.

The initial breeding process was shaky as many early attempts at creating a new breed resulted in dogs that had darker coats. This made them susceptible to being hunted and accidentally shot by people who thought they were something else. Fearing the concern for more accidents in the future that would entail more dogs being killed off, Russell opted to stick with a plan to go after a white coat that was actually distinguishable among others in the field.

The dog breed would be trained with the intention of trying to create the ideal hunting dog. Much of this training took place well after Russell's death. The dog breed was also carefully scrutinized as a means of making sure the breed would not have any serious health issues or defects. This came amid concerns in the late part of the nineteenth century that deafness was a problem that was found in many dogs at the time.

The dog would continue to be a working dog for generations as it would be used to lure out its prey in hunting situations and to search for different things in wide open fields. However, after World War II, the need for hunting dogs diminished dramatically. As a result, the Jack Russell Terrier would become more popular for being a companion dog or one that is appropriate for families. Some groups have gone as far as to breed the dog with other breeds like the Welsh Corgi among other small breeds.

Today the Jack is a dog that can be found as a working dog but it can also be enjoyable to have in larger fields. People from all around the world can enjoy these dogs although they tend to do their best in spots where they actually have more space to roam around in.

2) Classifications

The Jack Russell Terrier is not officially recognized by either the American Kennel Club or the Canadian Kennel Club. The AKC did consider adding the Jack to its listing of dogs in the 1990s but the Jack Russell Terrier Club of America, a group devoted to the breeding and preservation of the dog, refused. This was due to the club refusing to have the dog lose its working characteristics.

Disputes as to whether or not the dog will be recognized in the United States or Canada by their respective kennel clubs have been pervasive for a while. This has all come about in spite of the general popularity of the dog and how it has become so noteworthy over the years in terms of its stature and how it is built.

There are a few classifications that the Jack can be found in around the world. These include the following:

- The United Kennel Club, an American group that focuses on registering working dogs, listed the Jack as a Terrier.

- The Australian National Kennel Club has the dog in Group 2, a Terrier group.

- The New Zealand Kennel Club also recognizes the Jack as a Terrier.

- The FCI, or Federation Cynologique Internationale, is an international organization for dogs that focuses on Europe for the most part. The FCI has the Jack in Group 3 (Terriers) and Section 2 (Small Terriers). The dog is specifically listed at #345.

3) Colors and Types Available

The choices that people have when looking for the Jack Russell Terrier are typically going to be the same for the most part. This is thanks, in part, to how the dog was carefully bred with one specific hunting standard in mind over all these years.

Today the Jack Russell Terrier is typically found with a white coat with brown spots around its head and some other parts of its body. We will talk a little more about this point a little bit later on.

Some types of Jack Russell Terriers are ones that were bred with other small dogs. The Russell Terrier is one such example as its coat is slightly longer in length than what is found on a typical Jack Russell Terrier while its body is a little more rectangular in design. In other words, it may be difficult for you to actually find the Jack Russell Terrier that is in different types.

4) Other Interesting Things About the Breed

Every dog breed has its own features that make it stand out from all the others out there and the Jack Russell Terrier is not an exception. The Jack Russell Terrier is a breed that is unique in many special forms:

- The dog is known to be great for digging purposes.

- The dog is known to be relatively loud as it can bark quite often.

- The Jack Russell Terrier can jump at heights of about five feet or greater.

- It's also easy for the dog to go after smaller animals.

- There are no set points with regards to how the spots and other markings in the dog will look like. The dog can feature spots on its head and tail for the most part but some will also have these spots on their bodies. These include their main sides.

- This is one of the fastest dog breeds in the world as well. Some Jacks have been known to reach speeds of around 30 mph. These speeds can only be maintained for a rather short period of time though.

5) How the Dog Fits In With Your Health

As expressed in the last chapter, having a dog will be great for your health. The Jack Russell Terrier is one of the best dogs for you to check out with regards to your health. You need to be active if you want to stay healthy and fit; fortunately, the Jack just might be the perfect dog to have with this overall intention in mind.

The Jack Russell Terrier is very active and energetic. It will run around quite a bit and can move quite well in many open environments. It's a dog that will run around quite well and make you feel happy and energetic for quite a while.

A big part of the Jack Russell Terrier is that it is a breed that will especially be capable of sticking around with you and observe things around your body. This part about the Jack Russell Terrier is strong as its sense of smell has been honored over the years. It is strong thanks in part to the way it has been bred over all this time to find different things in wide-open fields. This sense of smell is a key part of why it is capable of identifying so many things with such ease.

6) Indoor or Outdoor Dog?

A great part of the Jack Russell Terrier is that it is a dog that can be found either indoors or outdoors. Still, that does not mean that the dog is comfortable in just any ordinary situation. The dog is a breed that can technically live indoors but it is best for you to keep the dog in an outdoor environment.

The Jack Russell Terrier has plenty of energy and will want to move around quite a bit. As a result, it is best for you to keep the Jack Russell Terrier outdoors. If the dog was indoors all the time then it would have far too much energy and become destructive.

This does not mean that you have to keep the dog outdoors all the time. After all, sometimes it can be dangerous for the dog to be outside during certain conditions where the weather is not all that conducive for outdoor activities.

The dog can be placed indoors for a good period of time during the evening hours. This should be around the time when the dog has gotten all its energy out.

7) Temperament

The temperament of the Jack Russell Terrier is one that shows just how energetic and active the dog is. The Jack Russell Terrier is one that is vocal and persistent. It has a fearless attitude and is quite willing to go anywhere.

The Jack Russell Terrier is intelligent enough to identify different things as it sees them. Think of this dog's attitude as a mix between being active and ready while also being smart enough to know what it is doing.

However, you should also know that the Jack Russell Terrier can be verbal. It is known to bark quite a lot throughout the day. This does not mean that it is a dog that will bark all day long.

Still, you should be rather careful when being around the dog as it can be verbal at times. The last thing that you'd want to bear with is a dog that might be overly vocal and is going to cause the neighbors to start complaining because that dog won't pipe down.

8) Behavior With Children

The Jack Russell Terrier is a good dog to have in your life but one thing that you should think about before bringing this dog home is your children. The dog is amazingly well-behaved around children but that doesn't mean that it will be great all the time.

A Jack will do quite well with children and will be very happy to be around them. It is just as energetic as those children. It loves to play and enjoy going outdoors.

This does not mean that the Jack is going to take just anything from children. As you read about in the last chapter, you should not keep a dog alone with children. This is especially the case with the Jack as it is a dog that will get upset if a child harms it.

Specifically, the Jack can become dangerous and will start to rough up children if it feels endangered. It will defend itself and may even try to bite someone. This is not always going to happen but there is always that realistic potential that something like this can happen. This is definitely not good in today's lawsuit-happy world.

The dog will be good around other children but that does not mean that you should just assume that a dog will stick around a child without any problems. You must talk with your children about the dog breed before allowing them to be around it. You might even want to share this guide with them.

Remember, make sure you always observe any children who are around the Jack so you can ensure that the dog will not attack. This breed loves kids but it has its limits.

9) Behavior With Other Pets

Like with children, the Jack is also good with other pets. It gets along with cats quite well and is also good around other dog breeds. Of course, one Jack can get along with other Jacks too.

Even with this in mind, there is still a potential for a Jack Russell Terrier to become aggressive if other pets are rough to it. It's a dog that is happy and positive but it is also one that is willing to go on the defense if it ever sees itself as being in danger of harm or being threatened in any particular way.

Specifically, you might want to see that a Jack Russell Terrier is socialized at an early age. It needs plenty of early exposure to other pets and people as it grows up. It has to understand that there is nothing for that dog breed to fear when it comes to being taken care of by other people.

In addition, as you will learn about a little later on, a Jack will typically do best when it is with another pet of the opposite gender. This will be discussed in detail a little later on.

It may also help to have the dog spayed or neutered just to ensure that it will not be at risk of engaging in further behaviors that might be dangerous to some.

10) Mixing With Indoor-Only Pets

There are many cases where some pets might have to be kept indoors. This is especially the case with many cats and some smaller dog breeds.

The Jack Russell Terrier is great to have as an outdoor dog that can also live indoors. However, you must be extremely careful if you're going to have your Jack in the same home as that of an indoor-only pet.

Although it's true that the Jack will get along with indoor pets, you have to watch out with regards to how the Jack will be treated. There are often times when your Jack might bring in debris and other materials from outside that can cause your indoor pet to become enticed. That pet will want to potentially try and run outdoors or become apt to trying and run out of the house to the point where it will be at risk of serious harm.

This is a dangerous concern that can come about with a Jack. However, if you make sure you clean off any debris that your dog gets into while outdoors and keep the process of going inside and outside your home as quick as possible then it should be easier for you to keep your dog safe.

Chapter 3: Vital Statistics of the Jack Russell Terrier

As you have learned so far, the Jack Russell Terrier is an amazing dog that is wonderful to be around. It is a bright and energetic dog that will certainly make for a good partner to have in your life.

You might be amazed at some of the different things that come around with regards to the Jack Russell Terrier. Let's take a look at a few of the important characteristics that you deserve to take a look at.

1) Country of Origin

The Jack Russell Terrier is a dog that comes from the United Kingdom. In fact, the British roots of the Jack go all the way back to the beginning of the Common Era. It was based loosely off of the Fox Terrier that was first observed by Romans in that part of the world around 50 BC.

Still, whether or not the origins of the Jack are totally within the UK remain a mystery. The one thing that is known for certain is that the Jack is a totally British dog when its upbringing in the nineteenth century is considered.

2) Litter Size

The Jack Russell Terrier will typically be from a litter size of about four to eight puppies. This depends on the health of the mother.

This is important to see if you wish to look for a female in the breed. You might have to consider spaying her if you want to ensure that she will not be at risk of giving birth to any further puppies. This is especially to make sure that she will not exhibit a substantial amount of aggressive behaviors over time.

There are some cases where the litter size might end up being a whole lot larger. These are rather extraordinary circumstances that are often hard to explain. The odds of a Jack giving birth to 24 puppies at once is extremely minimal but it's still a possibility. (Also, if a dog was to give birth to such a massive litter then it would probably have to go through a C-section at a vet's office and may not even survive the birthing process from all that pressure).

3) Height and Weight

The size of a dog is always important to see. The dog that you have can easily grow by quite a bit in its short life.

When compared with other types of dogs, the Jack is small in size. Specifically, a Jack Russell Terrier will vary in its size based on its gender.

A male Jack is going to be about 12 to 15 inches in height plus about 12 to 18 pounds in weight.

A female Jack will be 9 to 12 inches in height and 9 to 15 pounds.

This is a relatively small difference between the two. However, you may notice that their length is in proportion to their heights. Still, the difference between the male and female will not be all that easy to spot with the exception of some extreme cases where one dog is dramatically larger in size than the other.

On a related note, you can expect the dog to get to its full adult size within the first two years of its life. All Jacks will grow in their own ways but the size standard will always be consistent in terms of where they will end up.

4) Temperature

You must be aware of your Jack Russell Terrier's temperature at all times. Although you can easily keep the dog outside for an extended period of time, you must be extreme careful with regards to how it can handle certain extremes.

Specifically, the Jack Russell Terrier has an average body temperature of 101 to 102.5 degrees Fahrenheit or 38.3 to 39.2 degrees Celsius. This is a high range but it is something that must be checked carefully.

In fact, you can find a vet thermometer at a typical pet supply store right now. It can be very easy to use.

As it is a hunting dog, the Jack Russell Terrier is capable of surviving in some of the coldest conditions around. However, you might want to watch for how chilly it can get outside your home.

Don't bother keeping your dog outside in spots where it is 50 degrees Fahrenheit or 10 degrees Celsius. This is a condition where the dog can start to become bothered and could develop serious issues with its body.

The dog can last quite a while in many spots but it does not means that you should keep it outside all the time. Make sure you watch out when it comes to having your dog out in certain conditions.

Also, don't bother sticking the dog outside while it is raining or snowing. The dog may not be all that comfortable with those weather conditions.

5) Heart Rate

The dog's heart rate also has to be explored in detail as it is a sign of how active the dog might be but it can also be used as a sign of trouble if the heart rate is not healthy.

The heart rate will vary based on the dog's age. An adult's heart rate will go for about 60 to 160 beats per minute. The heart rate will clearly be much faster when the dog is exercising or if it has just stopped doing so. The slowest rate typically comes when the dog is sound asleep.

The heart rate is much greater for puppies. In particular, the dog's heart rate can be around 180 beats per minute.

Either way, the heart rate of the Jack is very different from a human's heart rate. Make sure you are fully aware of this when checking on whether or not your dog is healthy.

Sometimes you can feel the dog's heartbeat by placing your hand around the dog's chest or neck. It is often easier to determine a dog's heartbeat this way than it is to do this on another person.

You should particularly spend about 15 seconds measuring the dog's heart rate by putting your hand to its chest and then multiply the beats you are getting by 4. This should give you an approximate idea of what the dog's rate is.

Also, this should be measured when the dog is at rest. This will give you an ideal look into how well the dog's heart is beating.

6) Lifespan

A great part about the Jack Russell Terrier is that it has a good lifespan. The dog can live for about 13 to 15 years on average.

There is a potential that your Jack could live much longer than this. A good example of this can be found in a Jack named Willie who lived in the United Kingdom from 1994 to 2014. He lived to be 20 years and 106 days old. This is a record that was verified by the Guinness World Records group.

Of course, such extremes as Willie's case may be dramatic exceptions to the norm. In fact, there are actually two dogs in history that Guinness has confirmed to have lived to be at least 29 years of age! Still, if you take care of your dog the right way then there is a good potential that your dog will be around with you for years to come.

You should also see that your dog is from a healthy line. This might be a key in helping you figure out if the dog is at risk of illness and the potential to live a shorter life than what you might hope.

7) Intelligence

One of the best aspects of the Jack Russell Terrier comes from its intelligence. The dog is known to be rather bright.

Specifically, the dog has a keen intuition and is able to spot its master from many yards out. It also has a sense of smell that makes it capable of distinguishing many things that it sees out in a field. The ability of the dog to identify many of these points is an important aspect of the dog that everyone should take a closer look at.

It should be noted that the Jack Russell Terrier is not officially listed in the Intelligence of Dogs, Stanley Coren's famous review of dogs and how smart they are. This is due to the Jack not being officially recognized by the American or Canadian Kennel Clubs.

This dog should be easier to train than most other dogs thanks to its intelligence. Still, you will have to be persistent and patient with that in mind; you'll learn more about training your dog in a future chapter in this guide.

Chapter 4: Coat Colors and Types

One of the points about the Jack Russell Terrier that immediately makes it stand out from other dogs in the pack is that it features a coat that has a unique style to it. When paired with the overall frame of the dog, this coat will create a beautiful look that will make the dog a little easier to notice in any crowd.

The colors of the Jack Russell Terrier's coat deserve to be identified, as they are a key part of what makes the dog stand out from so many others out there. Specifically, the coat is not as long as you might expect.

1) Length

The Jack Russell Terrier has a short wire coat. Specifically, the wire coat is only an inch or so in length in many spots.

The coat is relatively easy to move through. Also, the dog should have a slight undercoat although it is not going to be all that long either. The coat is just there to insulate the dog and keep it as warm as possible.

The coat can be smooth in its texture for the most part. That is, if you move a comb through its coat then the dog's hair should be very easy to groom and treat.

Still, there are times when the coat might be rough and require a bit of effort to comb through. You might also find some broken hair bits here and there around your dog's coat at times but this is not a guarantee that such an issue will come about with your dog.

There are times when the coat might be a little closer to a medium length but this is not too common. Either way, you should not have to bear with having a coat that is too long or complicated on your dog's body. Anything that is easy to manage can be appealing and attractive for your care needs.

2) Color

The Jack Russell Terrier is white for the most part. In fact, at least

51 percent of the dog's body is expected to be white.

The markings that may be found on the dog's coat are tan, brown or black in color. Black markings are not all that common on these dogs but they are not a sign of anything overly unusual or ill-fitting with the dog. All three of these colors for the markings should be just fine.

Just take a look at any picture of a Jack Russell Terrier and you will notice that the dog comes in a standard white color and will feature many additional points to it that will make the dog look special. This is truly a dog that is different from what you might see elsewhere in the world.

The intensity of the tones that the dog has will vary by each individual dog as well. This makes the breed even more appealing in terms of its overall qualities and features.

3) Unique Markings

One positive aspect of the Jack Russell Terrier is that these dogs are unique in terms of how their markings are arranged. That is, it may be next to impossible for anyone to identify two dogs that are exactly the same in terms of their markings and other key features.

The markings that are found around the dog's body can be interesting to see. The Jack Russell Terrier is a breed that features spots that can be found all around different spots with the head being the key area that these can be found around.

These spots typically cover the dog's eyes and one or both of the dog's eyes. A blaze effect should be seen around the face.

A marking can also be found around the rear. This may be found at the base area of the tail for the most part. Sometimes it may be found at the end of the tail.

The marks that are on the main part of the dog's body can include little patches that go here and there around the sides. These marks can be rather attractive and beautiful for such a dog to spot.

These marks will typically be of the same color all around the dog's body. They are not going to change in terms of quality over time. There are times when the dog's spots might be in different colors but this is not all that common for people to see.

There are no set standards at dog shows in terms of how these markings have to be either. Then again, the guidelines for what does and does not fit in with the show standards that such a dog should have are unclear as not all organizations in the world are going to stick with the same standards for the overall appearance that a dog such as this needs to have in order to qualify to be a part of a show.

The dog should be white in its overall color but it should have plenty of nice spots that make it easily noticeable. These features will make the dog more attractive.

4) Smooth, Rough or Broken?

There are three critical points about a Jack's coat that you have to check on:

Smooth

A smooth coat for your Jack will go very close around the dog's body. It will not have trace hair parts on the head, legs, face or the main body. It will stick closely enough to where you might not have to use water to keep the coat from sticking out. This is a coat style that is recommended among dogs that might try to get into certain dog shows.

Rough

A rough coat will have an excess amount of hair all over the dog's body. The coat will be slightly longer in length although it will still be interpreted as a short-hair dog. In many cases the coat will be about one to three inches away from the dog's body. This should be relatively manageable during any grooming process but it will require a little more effort on your hand than if your dog had a smooth coat.

This coat is also softer in texture. This is not accepted by most dog shows.

Broken

A broken coat will be in the midway point between the smooth and rough coats. The trace hair will be found around the body and will not be likely to be visible around the head.

The broken coat style will not be as soft as it is for a rough coat. You will still have to regularly maintain it to ensure that the dog will continue to have a healthy look.

5) As It Ages

The dog's coat is not necessarily going to change in quality all that much as it ages. Like with any other dog, the coat is typically going to become a little rougher and maybe duller in color as it ages. This is a fascinating aspect of the dog that shows that it is going to be unique but will still vary based on how old one is.

The overall appearance and features of the Jack Russell Terrier will make it a very attractive dog for everyone to see. This handsome breed has many good features to it that makes it worthwhile in any home.

Chapter 5: Buying a Jack Russell Terrier Dog

The decision to have a Jack Russell Terrier should not be all that tough to make, what with the dog being so beautiful, smart and active. However, with so many Jacks out there, it can be a challenge for you to choose one.

This chapter is about helping you to understand the many key aspects that come with having a dog like this. It is a handsome and appealing dog but you should certainly be aware of what such a dog like this can be like before you stick with the commitment to having this dog in your home.

1) Pros and Cons Before You Buy

You need to be fully aware of the positive and negative aspects that come with the Jack Russell Terrier before you make a commitment to stick with this particular breed. These are considerations that deserve to be analyzed based on how the dog can behave in your home and how it can last for a while.

Pros

- A Jack will be very attractive and fun to have around your property.

- If you are trying to stay active in any manner then this dog will be great to have.

- The short coat means that it should not be all that hard for you to groom the dog.

- The small size of the dog also makes it so you might not have to worry about feeding it far too much. You'll still have the feed the dog on a regular basis, of course, but the process of doing so will be manageable.

- The Jack is a good watch dog that is active and ready to spot all sorts of things.

- This dog is also agile and active.

- It is an intelligent dog that knows what's around it.

Cons

- A Jack can be a little too active. In fact, it might be tough for you to get some rest on occasion when you consider just how active and excitable a dog like this can be.

- Sometimes a Jack can have an attitude of sorts when around other dogs. That is, the dog is not all that willing to be happy and positive to be seen as second to other dogs in the house.

- Jacks enjoy digging and could make a mess in your yard.

- Although it is smart, this dog breed can be excited enough to the point where it will want to try and do more to your home than what you might expect.

2) How To Choose the Right Puppy

There are many Jack Russell Terrier puppies for you to find these days. They come from many breeders and agencies and are different in so many ways. The differences between all of these puppies will make it to where you have to be careful as you find the right one. You need to be aware of a few critical points when taking a look at getting such a dog in your home:

Is the puppy expected to grow all that much?

You might want to see if there's information on the dog's family history with regards to how large the puppies can become. You need to know this so you can understand if the puppy that you are getting is going to grow to be relatively manageable in some way.

Is the puppy in a line that is healthy?

As you will learn about later on in this guide, the Jack Russell Terrier can be prone to some illnesses. While it is clear that breeders are trying their hardest to breed their dogs to where they will be easier to raise in many ways, you might want to take a look at how healthy one's line might be.

The problem with some dogs is that they might be prone to

illnesses if they are in lines that are filled with these particular problems. Fortunately, it should be easy for you to find a dog that you know will be safe to have as it will not be one that is likely to develop certain conditions.

What are the markings?

The markings on your dog are obviously not going to change much over time. Sure, the hair might start to gray up by a bit with age, but the markings will still be prominent. You should see that the markings on the dog that you are interested in are nice and appealing and will be worthwhile. Remember, it is not as though a dog can change its spots. Besides, sometimes these are features on the dog's body that will give it its own unique character.

How active is the puppy expected to be?

You might want to look at the puppy of interest to you in action. You need to see if that puppy is really active and willing to move around really fast and often. This is especially important if your yard or other place is not as large as it should be. You need to be prepared to see if the dog is actually going to be easy to handle without being harder to bear with than needed.

What has the breeder done?

You must make sure that the breeder you are getting in touch with has done more than enough to help take care of the dog and ensure that it will be healthy and comfortable around any person it comes near. Your breeder should have worked hard to socialize the dog, potentially train it and even ensure that it has gotten all of its necessary vaccinations.

Be sure to ask your breeder about what has to be done with the dog so you can be fully prepared. Considering the cost that comes with the process of taking care of special services for your dog, you might want to be on the cautious side of things.

3) One Dog Or Two?

While the Jack Russell Terrier can be a good dog to have in your home, you might want to be rather careful with regards to how you're going to have it around in your spot. The thing about the Jack Russell Terrier is that it is a dog that can be active and may end up trying to one-up a dog.

Your best bet is to start with one Jack Russell Terrier and then get that dog socialized well around other dogs. That is, the dog should be exposed to as many others as possible in the early parts of its life.

After this, it should be easier for you to get a second Jack in your home. This is often the best thing to do, as you want to ensure that the dogs in your home are going to actually get along with each other and understand their places in the household. The last thing you would want to bear with would involve the dogs fighting for your affection without knowing that you love them both.

It might also help to ensure that if you do have a second Jack that you have one that is of the opposite sex. One male and one female will be good to have in the home as they will both be comfortable with each other. They are not going to be as likely to fight as others that may be of the same gender. Be sure that you are fully aware of this when finding such dogs to have.

On a related note, it is best for only two Jack Russell Terriers to be kept together while unattended. Also, you should make sure they are of the opposite sex as Jacks of the opposite gender are not really all that willing to attack each other.

4) Best Age To Buy Your Puppy

It's typically best to buy a Jack Russell Terrier when it is about six to eight months of age. This might be relatively old by puppy standards but it's best for a number of reasons.

First, there is the need to get the puppy spayed or neutered. The puppy should be taken by a breeder or shelter to be spayed or neutered at the right time to ensure that it will not be at risk of engaging in overly rough and hostile activities.

However, the puppy cannot just be spayed or neutered right away. It is typically best to have it fixed about six months after its birth. This is to allow the dog to develop and to be at less of a risk of serious harm after the procedure is complete.

In addition, the puppy must be socialized for quite a while before it can be sent off. A professional who is going to sell the puppy to you must make sure that it is properly raised with socialization in mind.

On a related note, the puppy also has to be fed plenty of healthy foods as it grows. It needs to be near its mother and be fed by its mother during the first weeks of its life. This is crucial to the development of the dog as a failure to get the dog treated this way can be risky to its overall health.

Therefore, it is best to get your Jack Russell Terrier when it is at least six months of age. You need to be sure that it is primed for life and that it will easily develop over time. Failing to allow the dog to develop in some way can be dangerous in terms of how it is going to evolve.

Now, it is true that you could find a puppy that is as young as six to eight weeks of age. This might be a time to adopt a puppy that you might feel comfortable with but at the same time the puppy will be fragile and needs to be observed carefully to ensure it will not hurt itself in any way.

As mentioned earlier, you must be certain that you talk with the breeder about the specific dog. Don't ever assume that the dog will be one that's just safe to have no matter what.

5) Male or Female?

One of the best questions that many people have when it comes to buying any dog breed is if a male or female should be considered. Well, like with any other dog breed, a male Jack Russell Terrier will be larger in size than a female.

There is no correct answer to this question. You can stick with either a male or female. You should be aware of how these two are going to be different from one another.

Let's take a look at a few of the critical differences that can be found between male and female Jack Russell Terriers.

Males

- Males are typically a little more attentive to their masters.

- Males can also be more active and physically exuberant.

- There is less of a potential for a male to be moody and overly upset over time.

- You can ensure that a male will always be loyal to you.

Females

- Females are loyal but they can be reserved to themselves at times.

- Females are active but they are not going to be as likely to be rough.

- Females are often less likely to be distracted during the training process than males.

- Many of these females are also willing to have more of an interest in watching over their possessions or the environments that they are living in when compared with how the males act.

These are simple characteristics of males and females that both deserve to be compared with one another. It is fascinating to see how these two are going to act but it's critical for you to be aware of these points before buying a Jack Russell Terrier.

One point is for certain – if you already have one dog in your home then you should aim for a Jack that is of the opposite gender. A female will not be likely to wage any fights with a male. The male will then respect her decision and will not fight in any way. This is to keep a sense of peace in the relationship between these two dogs so the house can be comfortable.

It will be your own discretion as to whether or not you should have a male or female. Do be careful though when you are dealing with having more than just one Jack in the house.

6) Checking a Breeder

As great as a breeder can be when it comes to finding a Jack Russell Terrier, you need to be careful when checking on such an entity. There are a few things that you can do when looking into a breeder:

- See if the breeder is fully certified. Look to see what professional dog-related organizations it is a member of.

- Look at the environments that the dogs are kept in. They must be comfortable and wide open while being supportive and loving.

- Look to see what types of foods are being given to the dogs. They need to match up well with what we'll be talking about later on in this guide.

- Ask about the lineage records of the dogs that are at the breeder's place. Talk about things like when the mother has given birth, any known health-related issues that certain dogs have developed over time and so forth.

- On a related note, make sure the mother is healthy and is not being pressured into giving birth far too often. The mother should not be forced into giving birth more than twice.

- See if the dogs have received plenty of exposure to other dogs, people and other critical forms of stimuli. This is to ensure that the dogs will be properly treated with the right attention so they will know how to respond to others.

- Look for details on the immunizations and other medical-related forms of care that the dog has gotten.

- Be certain that the dog has also been spayed or neutered. Some breeders will do this for the dogs they have.

Most importantly, be sure that the breeder you get in touch with is one that has experience with the Jack Russell Terrier. In fact, it is better to stick with a breeder that only focuses on that one breed.

If you choose a breeder that is carefully focused on only one breed then it should be easier for you to have a dog that you know is healthy. In addition, you'll have one that came from a source that understands the many health and behavior-related needs that such a dog may have.

Always be certain when talking with a breeder that you're dealing with someone that understands the needs that your dog may hold. If a breeder cannot provide you with sensible answers to the questions that you might have then you may want to avoid dealing with that breeder.

7) Adopting a Dog

While you can often find a dog through a breeder that is devoted to the Jack Russell Terrier breed, you might want to think about the adoption process as well. Adopting a Jack can be a good option to consider but it is not without certain concerns.

Adoption agencies often take in dogs that have been left behind by their original owners. These dogs are left behind for many reasons:

- Their owners are no longer able to handle the financial requirements that come with having a dog.

- An owner might have also been abusive to the dog in some way. Sometimes an owner might have been sentenced to jail for a certain period of time as a result of one's actions.

- There are also times when someone might just drop off a dog and not do anything about it.

- There are some cases where a person cannot keep a dog due to the need to move to a new location where it would not be suitable for someone to have a dog in.

- Sometimes a dog is placed in an adoption agency's custody simply because the old owner has died and did not leave one's pet to anyone. In some cases the person who inherited the pet may not be capable of taking care of it, thus having to drop it off.

Adoption agencies often hold special drives at pet supply stores, community centers and other popular places. However, you need to be certain when finding adoption agencies that you think about these pointers when finding a dog:

- Take a look at the place that the dog is being taken care of in.

- Ask about any conditions relating to where a dog was found.

- See if the agency has any documentation on the dog based on things like what immunizations it had and if it has dealt with any health-related problems.

- Discuss any points on how well a dog is behaving. In some cases a dog that comes from a place where it was not taken care of properly may be dangerous and harmful to others.

Remember that an adoption agency will do plenty of good work and ensure that dogs that might have lost their way will get loving homes. However, be careful as a place that is as beneficial as this one may not have all the information that you want to get with regards to how a dog is being taken care of.

8) The Dangers of Puppy Mills

The puppy mill was a commonplace concept in the dog world a long time ago but it is dying off. This is because people have begun to discover that puppy mills are extremely dangerous.

A puppy mill is a place that will focus on trying to produce as many dogs as possible. This is all done with commercial gain in mind.

The puppies that you can find at such a place will typically be about 20 to 30 percent less in value than what you'd find at a traditional breeder. However, this reduction in value is often a result of the shoddy quality of life that these dogs go through.

The problems that come with puppy mills are vast:

- Puppy mills often don't have safe habitats for dogs to grow up in.

- These places are skip on quality in terms of care. They often feed the dogs cheap food and poorly made by-products.

- The dogs won't receive the proper socialization that they need either.

- Many of these dogs will not be checked upon to see if they are healthy.

- Sometimes the breeding process will go on without any regard to the potential health problems that some dogs can develop. For instance, a dog might be at risk of developing certain conditions if it comes from a line that has been bred at a puppy mill and was known to be unhealthy.

- The mother may be forced into giving birth many times in her life. This can be dangerous as a mother should only have two litters of puppies at the most in her life. Also, it is typically best to spend a few years in between litters so the mother can properly recover and actually nurse her newborns.

- The worst part is that sometimes these dogs are forced into breeding. This is regardless of whether or not they actually want to breed. (These dogs are not spayed or neutered either, thus keeping their extreme sexual urges intact).

Overall, puppy mills are extremely dangerous and harmful. You need to avoid doing business with such a place and stick instead with someone that is a little more caring.

Will They Be Safer Anytime Soon?

Puppy mills focus on profits instead of the welfare of the dogs that they are raising. Fortunately, some laws are being drafted as a means of regulating such places and making them more responsible.

These include many laws that require some commercial-based spots like puppy mills to be inspected on a regular basis. For instance, a puppy mill in Pennsylvania or Missouri must be inspected during the licensing process and once every year.

Meanwhile, many commercial breeders will have to pay fees with their local jurisdictions in order to stay operational. A kennel in North Carolina would have to pay $50 to be placed in the bidding to potentially be licensed to operate within the state.

Some places don't have such laws set up though. Some states like Florida, Kentucky and Nevada don't have any laws relating to puppy mills.

Some rules are also placed on the number of litters that can be produced. In the United Kingdom, a female can only be allowed to produce up to four litters in her life. She can only have one litter per year as well.

It is clear that there has been a good effort placed into trying to keep animals from being at risk at such places. Still, plenty of work has to be done to truly make them safe. Therefore, you are better off sticking with breeders that focus on the Jack or through adoption agencies that may offer support.

9) Dog Shopping List

The decision to buy a Jack Russell Terrier should not be all that hard for you to do. The big question is to see if you are prepared for getting the things that the dog will need as you bring it home. There are several things that have to be used in your dog shopping list so you will be ready when the dog actually comes in.

Buckle Collar

A good collar should be made of a material that is comfortable and will not stretch, thus ensuring that it will not slip off easily.

ID Tag

An ID tag should be used on the dog's collar. It can include the dog's name and address as well as your contact information. This is important, as you need to be certain that the dog can be tracked in the event that it ever becomes lost for any reason.

Leash

A leash needs to be made with thick leather materials and also have a good and long body that is easy to handle. Look for a good grip on it so you will easily hold onto it without being at risk of having it slip off of your hand.

Crate

A crate should be used so you can keep the dog from running off. The crate can protect the dog and make sure it is not going to escape your grasp. Don't keep the dog in there for more than three to five hours at a time though. The last thing you'd want is for your Jack to become upset or nervous.

Bowls

You should have two bowls for your dog. One is for water and the other is for food. Keep them together but don't make them too close to the point where the water will spill into the food bowl or vice versa.

Keep the bowls a few inches from each other. Take about six inches as it will be good enough distance without taking up far too much space.

If you plan on having multiple Jacks in the home then make sure you train the dogs to follow through with their own bowls. Train each dog separately to eat by presenting them with bowls that feature specific colors or other markings on them. Anything that can be done to show differences in whatever you have available will always be worthwhile.

On a related note, it is best to keep the dogs from drinking out of the same water dish. Try and use two separate food bowls and two separate water bowls if you have two different dogs in the house. This is to ensure that there are no fights over who gets what and also so the dogs will be comfortable with each other.

Grooming Materials

Regardless of the quality of the dog's coat, you need to be certain that you are careful when doing so. You will need to gather plenty of different grooming items to make the process of caring for the dog as easy to handle as possible.

A good brush and comb can be great as well as clippers for the dog's claws and even a fine shampoo that has been formulated for the Jack's coat. We'll go over the art of grooming later on in this guide.

Appropriate Toys

There are many kinds of toys that you can get right now to entertain your dog. You can choose from options like tennis balls and traditional chew toys to rawhide bones. The choices for you to enjoy will be great to have in your home.

In fact, these toys will not only allow your Jack Russell Terrier to become active but they will also allow the dog's energy to be let out quite well while indoors (you should still supervise the dog to see that it is not tearing up stuff in your home though).

In addition, some of these toys can help to build the dog's jaw muscles and teeth so they will all be healthy and well-built. This is particularly the case with some of the thicker and sturdier options around.

The best part of these dog toys is that you can find an extended variety of options. If you're looking for a toy that the dog can just grab and chew then that will work. If you want something that you can throw so the dog can retrieve it and bring it back to you then that will be perfect as well.

Dog License

We will talk in detail about getting a dog license later on in this guide. It will be critical for you to have such a license to ensure that your dog will be properly behaved and less likely to be hostile or angry in some way.

For starters, you should know that a dog license will be an important document to have. This ensures that you are fully listed as the legal owner of the dog. It is a consideration that must be used in accordance with the law depending on where you live. It is not hard to get a license but you must make sure you get it as soon as you have a dog (assuming you require one).

Be aware that the things that were listed here should not be interpreted as a totally comprehensive list of things for you to get for your dog. Feel free to talk with your veterinarian for information on all the things that you could get for your dog.

This will be discussed later but you should talk with your local government as to whether or not you do need a license for your dog. There is a potential for you to receive a fine in the event that you do not have a license for your dog and something troublesome comes about for whatever reason because your dog did something in a local area.

10) Puppy Proofing Your Home

It can be exciting to bring home your Jack Russell Terrier for the first time. However, that does not mean you should just get ready and present that dog in your home right away.

You have to be fully aware of what you are going to do with the dog before anything else can be done. Your dog, like any other animal, is going to be curious when it enters into your home. It will see lots of stuff that it has never experienced in the past and as a result will practically play around and goof off with all the things that you have.

You must make sure you puppy-proof your home. This is a process that entails protecting spots in your home to ensure that the puppy will not be at risk of harm as it comes home. If you prepare your home the right way then your puppy will be safe...and even that is a challenge to pull off in its own right.

You might be amazed at the hazards that can come about in your home. However, there are many things that can be done right now to keep your dog protected when it comes home. Here's a look at what to do right now:

- Keep any foods you have in your home locked up so the dog will not try and eat them.

- Install locks on cabinets if necessary. Specifically, you should add locks on the ones that the Jack can actually reach. This is due to how the dog can be smart enough to where it could potentially break into a cabinet and steal stuff from it.

- Keep all bathrooms secure. Specifically, the toilet bowl should be kept down. In fact, you should probably close the doors to all your bathrooms when no one is using them.

- Use small caps around the electric plug outlets. These caps can be inserted into those plugs to keep them from being exposed. This ensures that the plugs will not be open and available for a puppy to stick its paw or nose in.

- Keep any chemicals in your spot as far away from the dog as possible. In addition to locking up items that may be hazardous, you must also place them in spots that would be inaccessible to the dog.

- Keep all electric wires out of the way. Make sure they are secured on walls or on corners of the house that your dog is not going to get into.

- Keep any plants in your home as far from the dog as possible. Also, if there are any plants in your home that may be interpreted as being poisonous then you should throw them out as soon as possible.

- Be sure you sweep or vacuum your home before bringing the puppy home. You do not want to have the puppy become ill because of some of the stuff that might be lying around your home.

- If there are other people in the same home as you then be sure you talk with them about your plan to have a dog in the home. This is regardless of whether this is the first one you've got or if you want to have a second or even a third in your space.

You should spend plenty of time securing all that stuff in your home before the Jack comes home. Don't ever think that your Jack is not going to get in any trouble. The odds are your new Jack is going to be curious about the stuff that is in your home and might end up getting into some kind of trouble.

11) The First Weeks With the Puppy

You must make sure that you are careful when getting your puppy taken care of at the start. The puppy must be taught plenty of things about living in your home. This is especially the case with a Jack Russell Terrier as this dog is one that might be a whole lot smarter than what you might expect out of it.

Show Who's In Charge

You have to show the puppy that you are the one who is the head of the house. You may not be a fellow dog but you can always show that you are the most powerful person in the home and that the dog should be paying attention to you.

There are many things that can be done to show your dog that you are the one who is responsible for calling the shots in a space.

Praise Quickly

Don't think that you can give lots of love and praise to the dog. Be swift and careful when giving it praise for doing things right. Say something good and then move on. The key is to show that you are the one who is responsible for determining whether whatever is happening in a spot is positive and worth getting into.

Punish Quickly

You also have to give out any punishments that might come about as quickly as possible. Be swift in these and keep from showing extreme anger or other negative feelings and the dog will see that you are in charge.

Give Permission At the Right Times

If the dog wants to go outside then make sure the dog does something positive that encourages you to allow the dog to go outside.

Don't just act as though the dog can do what it wants. Let the dog wait for a bit and see how it can learn a desired behavior of sorts. If the dog can learn this in time then it should be easy for the dog to be ready to do things right and without any arguments.

Don't be afraid to deny permission to your dog either. As much as a Jack might want to try and get its way in some form, you have to be certain that you aren't too aggressive in terms of mounting control over the dog.

Take a look at how your dog behaves and make sure you explain to your dog what behaviors are desired and what should be ignored. This is to see that nothing wrong will come about when trying to get your dog to listen to you.

Be Calm and Confident

As the leader of the house, your dog is going to easily pick up on your behaviors. Show that you are calm and willing to do what you can to make yourself feel positive. If you do this then the dog will be less likely to feel stressed and therefore more likely to actually listen to what you have to say.

Remember that you are the one who will be in charge of all the stuff that goes down in the home. Make sure you act like you know that you are in total charge of all that you see and observe.

The First Night

The first night with your new Jack Russell Terrier can always be tough. That's because the dog can be so unpredictable in terms of how it is going to behave. You have to think carefully about what will go along during that first night when the dog is not aware of what is in your home.

Naturally, this is a time when the dog might feel nervous or worried. This is because the dog is away from its family and in your home for a change. The Jack may become worried and uncertain about what will come about in the home. It is a truly unfamiliar place that the dog may not enjoy being in.

That's where you are going to come into play. You need to express a sense of control and discipline in your life so you will feel as happy and comfortable about yourself as possible.

You need to make sure the puppy is in a spot that is comfortable during that first night. You might hear the puppy whimper or whine at times but the puppy will become less likely to do this when it feels happy and comfortable with whatever is going on in an area.

Allow your puppy to feel relaxed and don't leave it alone for an extended time. You need to show that you are someone that the dog will be comfortable and easy to be around.

It may also be a smart idea to have plenty of different blankets or other items to keep a dog warm in. Think of it as though the dog would have its own bed. This especially ensures that the dog will be less likely to jump on your bed and sleep there.

You also have to be aware of how the dog will want to try and use the bathroom at certain times. It's always smart to bring the dog out to an open space to ensure that it will not be at risk of having some kind of accident in your home.

Be polite and courteous as you let the dog out to an area to use the bathroom as the dog will eventually begin to associate a particular part of the home as a place where it will be safe to go into when trying to use the bathroom.

Your dog will need to be kept in a spot that it is comfortable in so you will not have it move around and potentially become ready to move around the house. You can always start keeping the dog at one space in the home and then expand the areas of the home that the dog can go into gradually. You might have to spend a few days to allow the dog to go through the entire home but it will be worthwhile as the dog will feel a little happier and more comfortable with the entire home as it moves through.

Most importantly, you need to present a clean and healthy home at all times. Show that your home is a place that the dog will be comfortable in. Don't ever be overly angry or upset and make sure you are as inviting as possible so the dog will feel welcome in your home.

The First Week

As mentioned just now, opening up the house to the dog should be done on a gradual basis during the first week with it in the house. Your Jack Russell Terrier is going to be very inquisitive so make sure you are cautious when getting the place opened up.

You must start by opening up the spot in the home where the dog will use the bathroom first. The area with the door that will lead to the yard spot where the dog will use the bathroom in should be opened up first. This is to allow the dog to feel comfortable and ready for whatever may come about in a yard.

This is a very important point that needs to be done as you let the dog move around the home. Don't ever assume that you can just allow the dog to come around different spots of a home here and there.

Make sure the dog is also stimulated with plenty of chew toys and other things to do around the home. Don't ever let the dog go unsupervised either. The Jack needs to be aware of what is and is not interpreted as positive behavior. This is to see that the dog will not engage in activities that might potentially become harmful and dangerous.

Make sure you prepare plenty of spots for the dog to eat and use the bathroom in. You have to get the dog to learn exactly where one should be going when it comes to using the facilities in your home and for eating. The goal is to create a sensible series of concepts for the dog to follow to allow it to actually understand where it should and should not be going in your home.

12) Common Mistakes To Avoid

As great as it can be to have a dog in your home, you have to be rather careful with regards to how it will behave. Specifically, you must avoid a few mistakes that many new dog owners make. These are mistakes that can especially be a hassle when it comes to having a Jack Russell Terrier in the home. Interestingly enough, some of these mistakes are ones that people often misinterpret as positive things to do with their dogs.

Sleeping In Your Bed

We have all seen those pictures of dogs sleeping in the beds of their masters. We see them as endearing as they show just how much a dog loves its master. The fact that such a bed can be warm for the dog to enjoy being in can be just as important to see.

However, it is not a good idea to allow a Jack Russell Terrier to sleep in your bed. There are many problems that can come about as a result of letting a dog like this sleep there. It's obviously not good because the dog can cause damage to the bed at times. The dog may also infringe upon your privacy. More importantly, you might find it relatively hard for you to actually get to sleep after a while.

There are a few things that you can do to keep your dog from sleeping in your bed:

- Create a spot that your dog can sleep in. Establish an area in the home that the dog should be placed in at night and make it as comfortable as possible. Keep that area quiet and warm so the dog will feel happy.

- Train the dog to sleep at its spot at night by offering treats and other incentives to encourage the dog to stay there. Try to use the word "bed" to associate this point so the dog will be more likely to actually sleep there.

- Be gentle to the Jack as you push it off the bed. Don't be aggressive; instead, gently pick up the dog and use a simple request to the dog to ask that it is not going to get in the way of the bed any further.

Remember, a sleeping spot for your Jack should be one that is comfortable and easy for the dog to enjoy being on. Keep it comfortable and easy and the dog will be happy.

Picking Up the Dog At the Wrong Time

Just because a Jack Russell Terrier looks pretty and cute does not mean that you should be picking it up every single time. You need to think about when you are going to pick up the dog. You must make sure the dog is comfortable around you and that you are not going to be at risk of bothering it.

Make sure you don't pick up the Jack Russell Terrier if it is overly agitated or active. The dog will become upset and angry if you bother it. Be sure you see how quickly the dog is moving or if it is overly active so you can get an idea of whether or not the dog is comfortable around you.

Playing Too Hard or Too Long

Your Jack Russell Terrier will be active and willing to do whatever it wants out in the field. You must not play far too hard with your dog or else it will start to feel at risk of being harmed or injured in some way.

Make sure you are gentle with your Jack Russell Terrier or else the dog will be at risk of serious problems. Also, be sure that you stick with playing sessions that are about ten to thirty minutes on average. The last thing you want to do is cause your Jack to wear out rather quickly. You need to keep the Jack happy and less likely to feel overly stressed out for any reason.

You also need to keep from playing hard because the dog might also become overly tired. As energetic as the dog is, it can be tough to have around in a spot.

Hand Play

Hand play is an activity where you let your Jack Russell Terrier play around with your hand, allowing the dog to bite it or scratch it among other things. The Jack will think of your hand as some sort of toy at the start of its life because it may not fully understand you in some way.

This is not necessarily the best thing to consider when it comes to taking care of your dog but you have to be fully aware of how the dog will do this. Most dogs do this as a means of being all playful. However, there also comes a time when a dog will do this because it is afraid of something that might be in a spot.

It is important to train your Jack to stop biting or mouthing around your hand. You need to be gentle when the Jack is about to start doing this. Make sure you politely warn the dog about not playing around with your hand as it is outreached in any manner. Don't ever let the dog think that it is okay to just go out and bite on your hand.

Besides, it can be important for you to get your dog to stop doing such a thing. The last thing you want to deal with is your dog accidentally biting down hard enough to the point where you might actually start bleeding.

Distraction and Replacement

The idea of distraction and replacement sounds simple. It involves getting your dog to look at something and then replacement an item in a room that was in the dog's possession with something new. This is done as a means of keeping the dog from harming anything in your home that might be of value to you.

For instance, if the dog is biting on a newspaper then you could distract the dog and replace it with some other chew toy.

This is an interesting concept but the fact is that a dog, especially a Jack Russell Terrier, will often be smarter than you might think. It will not take much for the dog to spot the difference between the new and old items.

You should not try to distract and replace items that are in the dog's vicinity. Instead, you need to train the dog to avoid playing with the stuff that you don't want it to be around.

13) Bonding With Your Dog

It is essential for you to know how to bond with your dog the right way. Your dog is going to be a great partner in your life and as a result you need to see that you're doing what you can to bond with your dog.

Specifically, you need to show that you are a friendly person to be around. The dog has to be trusting of you in order to ensure that your relationship with the dog will be as strong as possible.

There are many things that you can do in order to bond with your dog and make the relationship that you have better:

- Spend a little more time with your dog. Show your dog that you will always be there.

- Take care of the dog training activities on your own. Be there to show the dog that you understand the needs that the dog holds when it comes to learning.

- Be willing to stay playful and enjoyable.

- Understand how your dog behaves and responds to different activities. You need to be aware of how your dog is going to behave in all sorts of special situations.

Remember that you need to be gentle when bonding with your Jack Russell Terrier. The key is to show that you are a caring person that the dog will love to be around and will not be threatened by in any manner. This is to ensure that the dog will be happy around you and comfortable by all means.

Chapter 6: Costs

You obviously have to pay money to have a dog. This comes from not only the cost associated with actually acquiring the dog but also the cost of the stuff that you'll have to use while taking care of your dog.

The cost that comes with having a dog will entail many points relating to care and the materials to use. These are great things to find but if you think about the costs associated with the Jack Russell Terrier then you might find that it is not going to be all that hard for you to find something of value.

The important thing about the Jack Russell Terrier and its cost is that you won't have to spend too much money when compared with other dog breeds, what with the dog being a small breed. Still, that does not mean that having a dog in your home is a minor investment.

It will cost quite a bit of money to have the dog around but it will be worthwhile when you consider the many positive things that can come about in your life as a result of having such a dog in your home. You must be prepared when you are bringing in such a dog.

1) Cost To Buy

The cost of the Jack Russell Terrier is the first point to explore. The cost can be rather high depending on where you go.

The average cost of a Jack Russell Terrier can go for about $1,200/£800. This is a high value but it is a typical one that many breeders will charge for dogs who are very healthy and attractive.

You might find some places that will go down to $800/£540 for the dog. This might sound more appealing but you must be aware of the potential reason as to why the dog is more affordable at this point. In some cases it might come from the dog being treated differently or because the dog might have some hereditary concerns that might manifest themselves over time.

Some places will charge more for dogs that could be accepted at certain dog shows in different parts of the world. These include spots that might charge at least $2,000/£1,300 on average for your Jack Russell Terrier. Be careful though as those dogs are ones that are specifically bred to be out at different shows.

Naturally, you can always go to a rescue agency to adopt a Jack Russell Terrier. Be aware though that just because a dog is a rescue does not mean that it is going to cost any less. Sometimes the charges may be the same due to the need to ensure that the pets being taken care of are actually being handled and treated the right way.

Also, you could possibly go to some classified ad website to find deals on the dog that entail paying much less. Still, you should be cautious as sometimes a good deal might be available but it may be at a cost – perhaps the person selling you the dog is unaware of certain medical issues that it might have developed or the dog did not get its proper vaccinations among other things that it requires in order to stay healthy.

2) Regular Cost Of Owning a Dog

The initial cost of having a Jack Russell Terrier might be high to some but it's important to also know about the regular cost that comes with having a dog. There are many things that you might have to pay for over time.

A quick note: The cost of having a Jack Russell Terrier may not be as great as it might be when compared with a much larger dog. This is due to the dog not requiring as much food as a larger one or the dog being a whole lot easier to maintain and take care of at different times.

You may want to keep a tally of these points. Not all processes are required but some of them are necessary or at least recommended.

An additional note: These points are for many of the basic essentials that you'll require for your dog. There are other dog-related services out there that you can use that might also cost money. From dog-walking services to pet spas, you might be surprised at the extensive variety of dog-related things that are out there for you to check out.

Spaying/Neutering

The cost to spay or neuter a Jack Russell Terrier will be around $200/£135. This is much less than it is for dogs in larger breeds and in some cases a breeder might have already taken care of this cost for you.

Make sure you ask a breeder about whether or not a dog that you want has actually been spayed or neutered beforehand though so you can determine if you do need to take the dog in for this procedure.

A quick note: We will talk about spaying and neutering later on in this guide. This is a critical procedure to take care of when it comes to keeping your dog healthy and happy. It is not required among pet owners to do but considering the benefits that come from it, it is strongly worth the investment.

Food

The cost of food should be rather predictable. A Jack Russell Terrier will not eat as much food as a larger breed. Therefore, this should keep you from having to spend too much.

It can cost about $70/£47 to take care of the dog's food every year. This might increase if you stick with some high-end options for your dog to enjoy. (In fact, some companies actually make dog food products that have to be chilled. And let's not forget about those "ice cream for dogs" products!)

This cost is for dog-specific foods. You could technically give the dog certain foods that people normally eat (which we will discuss later) but you must be extremely careful as there are some that the dog must also avoid having at all times (another point that we will talk about too).

Toys

You might expect to pay around $40/£27 on toys for your dog each year. You might think that you can get a toy and the dog will have it for a while but the truth is that a toy can easily wear out as the dog chews on it. It will eventually get to the point where the dog will not actually get any kind of enjoyment out of the toy it was originally playing with. You will have to get a replacement for the toy at this point.

Some toys can be a little more elaborate though. These include toys like special types of furniture sets that dogs can jump up and down on.

Vet Care

Your dog needs to be taken to a vet's office at least once a year. You could even take your Jack Russell Terrier to the vet twice in a year if you really feel a need for doing so. You have to bring your dog out to the vet to ensure that it is being taken care of the right way.

A veterinarian will not only check on the Jack's health but also offer regular treatments for heartworm, fleas and other commonplace issues. Your vet can also help with the spaying or neutering process.

Your vet care costs can get to be around $200/£135 per year. This can be based on the charges that come with traditional checkups with your vet.

Again, this is a lower price than what it can cost for large breeds; a larger breed might incur charges that are about a third higher than what a small breed like the Jack might entail.

Pet Insurance

You are not required to have pet insurance on your Jack Russell Terrier. However, it is recommended that you have it anyway. Pet insurance allows you to stay protected against the costs that might come about when it comes to emergency medical bills for your dog.

Reports by the American Society for the Prevention of Cruelty to Animals states that the average cost for pet insurance is around $225/£150 per year.

There is no way how you can directly figure out the exact cost of pet insurance for your particular Jack Russell Terrier as every dog will have its own value with regards to how much it can be insured for. You might have to pay more based on the age of the dog. The cost might also be high if your dog is in a spot like an urban area where the potential for that dog to be injured will be greater.

Also, the cost from each insurance provider will vary. Many providers are willing to charge different amounts of money for their insurance plans.

Like with any other insurance policy, you must also be aware of the coverage points that come around in the policy that you take.

Grooming

It's often best for you to work on grooming your dog on your own. This is because you could potentially save quite a bit of money on the cost of grooming your dog when you take care of it yourself.

Specifically, grooming can cost at least $200/£135 per year on average. This is due to not only the cost of the supplies and materials needed for taking care of grooming (nail cutters, shampoo products, brushes and combs, heat-free air dryers, etc.) but also for the possible personal assistance that someone might provide you.

These costs can even include the charges associated with getting a dog's teeth cleaned. It can cost about $15/£10 to get a toothbrush for your Jack. These charges are included in the process of getting the dog taken care of.

Of course, grooming the dog on your own is best if you want to keep the dog healthy. In fact, the grooming process will be discussed in detail soon in this guide.

The overall cost of the dog can become very high. You have to be fully aware of this point if you want to have a dog as it can cost thousands over the years to have your dog.

3) What Will the Overall Cost Be?

The overall cost of the dog will vary based on what you do with it. The dog can cost quite a good deal of money to have in your home but if you understand what you will be doing with your pet then you might find it to be rather easy for you to feel great with having one around.

It could cost at least $1,000/£670 per year to have a Jack Russell Terrier in your home. This is when all those considerations for medical care, grooming items, toys, foods, and other things are considered. Seeing how you would have to multiply this total by at least 12 on average – one for every year that the dog is around for – and you would end up getting into the five-digit range in terms of the overall cost of your dog.

Just remember – the total cost of the dog will vary heavily based on the condition of that dog and what you choose to get for it. This chapter is simply a guide that gives you an idea of what to expect out of the dog that you want to have.

Chapter 7: House Training

The process of training any kind of dog can be a challenge in its own right. You might think that you know how to take care of a dog but the truth is that sometimes the dog might be testing you in the training process.

This chapter is about how to train a dog to handle different spots in your home. There will be a chapter later on in this guide that is devoted to teaching your dog how to handle different commands and to obey whatever you say to it. For now, let's talk about the house training practices that can be used.

1) Human Training

Human training is a process that can be complicated to some but it's easy to understand when you really think about it. This is a practice that entails getting your dog to recognize you.

You have to make sure the dog recognizes you if you're going to make any training process work right. If your dog is not aware of who you are then it might be a challenge for you to actually train that dog and keep it happy.

It might help for you to use dog treats and associate them with you. In particular, you might want to provide the dog with treats for when you ask for it to come to you. If the dog comes to you, offer a simple treat. Let the dog know that the treat is correlated to you. That is, the dog will become a little more attached to you if you just show that you care about it.

Make sure you are also gentle and comfortable around the dog. Don't be too rough around the dog; instead, show that you are someone who can be trusted.

If you are good around the dog and as gentle as possible then it should be very easy for the dog to feel better around you.

2) Bell Training

Have you ever heard about the old Pavlov study about the dog responding to a bell with a certain stimuli? This is one of the most noteworthy scientific studies to have ever taken place. Amazingly enough, it is also a study that has proven itself to be a great training method.

In fact, you can use this training process to help teach the dog how to ask to go outside in order to use the bathroom. This will make accidents less likely to happen within your home.

Here's a look at what you can do in order to make the bell training process as easy to handle as possible.

1. Show the dog the bell.

2. Give the dog a treat if it touches the bell. Make sure you condition the dog to want to touch the bell when it sees it.

3. Show the bell again and only give it a treat if the dog actually touches the bell.

4. Hang the bell around the door that the dog would have to go through in order to get to a spot outside to relieve itself.

5. Place a treat outside the door and then see that the dog will touch the bell. Only give the dog that treat if the dog actually rings the bell. Give the dog the treat by opening the door and letting the dog go after it.

6. The next time you see the dog as it appears to have a need to use the bathroom, point at the door and bell.

7. Let the dog ring that bell once more.

8. After the dog is done ringing the bell, open the door let the dog use the bathroom. Give the dog a treat after this is fully done.

9. Make sure you only open the door after the dog rings the bell in cases when the dog appears to have a need to use the bathroom.

This is a practice that will allow the dog to associate the bell with something that allows it to go outside the use the bathroom. The Jack Russell Terrier might be at risk of having accidents in your home if you do not teach it how to use this bell.

3) Kennel Training

Kennel training is a practice that is also known as crate training. This is typically used as a means of helping your dog to become aware of how a kennel works. It can be essential to teach your dog about this because you will certainly have to use your kennel at times when the dog has a need to go to the vet.

In addition, kennel training can also help you teach the Jack Russell Terrier about the spot one should go into when it is time to sleep or when there is a thunderstorm and the dog might get overly excited about what's outdoors. It's a great practice that will encourage protective thinking for your dog.

Here's a look at how to take care of the practice:

1. Call the dog over to the crate.

2. Give the dog a treat after it comes over.

3. Give the dog a command for entering into the kennel.

4. Praise the dog and then give it a treat as it enters into the kennel. Close the door at this point.

5. Let the dog in the kennel for about five to fifteen minutes. This should be enough to allow the dog to become a little more used to the kennel area.

6. Let the dog out after that time period has gone by.

7. Allow the dog to come back to the crate only when it feels comfortable in doing so. Make sure you give the dog a treat to associate the area with positive things.

8. You can expand upon the time for when the dog is to stay in the crate. You can even leave the crate door open provided that you watch for how the dog is to act in that area.

This is a great practice that will teach the dog to get into this proper space and become comfortable with it. The Jack Russell Terrier will be less likely to fear it as well.

You should be rather cautious when getting the Jack Russell Terrier into this spot though. Don't ever leave the dog locked in there for too long and don't leave it unattended for a while as you train it. You need to see that the Jack will actually respond well to the training process.

This is a process that can also work for when you're trying to get your dog to move into a larger exercise pen. In particular, you can have the dog come to the exercise pen with the right prompts and treats as a means of ensuring that there's a positive connotation between the pen and the dog. This is useful considering how an exercise pen is a large spot that will allow the dog to have more than enough space to move around without feeling trapped or stuck in an area.

4) Apartment Training

Just because you are in a smaller apartment does not mean that the Jack Russell Terrier cannot be found in your place. You can train your dog to live in your apartment with a few ideas in mind.

1. Train your Jack to know how to respond to people the right way.

You specifically have to train your Jack to ensure that the dog is not going to be at risk of barking at other people or even at random. The key is to ensure that the dog learns prompts to be quiet and that it will not keep everyone at an apartment complex up. You can learn more about training your dog to be quiet a little later on in this guide.

2. Train the dog to behave around other dogs in the area.

The odds are you might be in dog-friendly apartments and as a result come across loads of other dogs in the area. This might be fun for your dog and will provide you with plenty of options for socialization with other people. However, you have to be careful when it comes to training the dog around others. You have to specifically make sure you train the dog to where it will behave around other dogs just fine.

As mentioned earlier, the Jack is a dog that will interact with other dogs quite well provided that it has been socialized with them at an early age. You must make sure that you allow the dog to interact with others at an early age so the dog will not become fearful.

Make sure you also watch for how your Jack Russell Terrier responds to the situation it has gotten into when with other dogs. If you ever see your Jack's body stiffening or the tail being tucked around the time the dog interacts with another then it might be best to head out. You need to ensure that the dog will not get into any worse of a situation in the event that it begins to feel nervous.

5) Free Training

Free training is a practice that entails teaching the dog where it can and cannot go in a field. You have to be careful when training your dog with regards to where it can and cannot go.

While it's true that an electric fence and associated collar might be ideal to have, this is not always going to work as well as you might hope. There's also that concern that comes with the ethical standards for the fence. The dog should not be harmed when such a fence is to be used but even some people may refuse to have such a fence in an area just as a means of keeping one's dog protected.

You need to establish a series of parameters for your yard and a signal to let the dog know where it is allowed. One option to consider is to take the dog for a walk around your yard.

Show the dog around different spots in the yard. Try and show the spot that it should go to the bathroom at.

If the dog walks into a spot that it is not allowed to get into then a gentle tug on the collar can help. This should drive the dog away from the unwanted spot. A small bit of force will be used here but it will be relatively minimal.

Whatever you do in this situation, do not tug extremely hard at the collar. A small bit of force may get the dog to notice that it should avoid a certain spot and will have that spots links in one's mind to the feeling of discomfort. However, if you are aggressive and end up possibly hurting the dog then that dog will not feel like it wants to be around you.

Remember, this is a process that is more than likely going to be more affordable than having an electric fence. You might think that the electric fence is a good idea but there are too many problems attached to it. The collar that a dog will wear in conjunction with the fence might weigh quite a bit and may wear off in terms of its power, for instance.

Also, the cost of the electric fence may be out of your reach. You might spend $700/£475 on a fence in your home or maybe even more depending on what you need to have in your space.

Chapter 8: Grooming

Grooming is the key part of what makes a Jack look so beautiful.

The best part of grooming is that it does more than just make your Jack appealing. It can also give you plenty of time to spend with your dog. This in turn makes it easier for the dog to be a little more trusting in you. Your dog will feel more comfortable around you when you clean it properly.

Of course, some people like to place their own unique styles on their dogs. This is all to your discretion but the key of grooming is to make your dog feel happy and look great.

In addition, if you know how to groom your dog then you will not have to worry about spending money on expensive professional treatments. You might find that it will not cost as much for you to get all these items for grooming when compared with what it would cost for a typical dog grooming process.

For instance, you might find that a professional grooming service can cost around $50/£33 to handle. This is just one session of grooming as well.

Meanwhile, the cost of various materials that you'd use for grooming your dog will be much less when you consider how you can use all of these for multiple grooming sessions in your own home. A brush may be about $5/£3 on average while it can cost $10/£6 for a bottle of shampoo. Meanwhile, a heat-free dryer can cost at least $40/£24 to get. Nail cutters can also be found for at least $10/£6 each.

In addition, will be easier for you to be familiar with your dog's body. This is important in that there is always that potential for a dog to develop lumps or other problems around its body. These are problems that might be signs of extremely serious medical conditions.

The grooming process is important for when you are trying to get your Jack Russell Terrier to look great. With all this in mind, let's talk about what you can do to groom your Jack the right way.

1) Bath Time

You have to give your Jack Russell Terrier a bath on occasion. The problem with any dog is that it can get into plenty of dirty spots. This is especially the case for a dog that has a propensity to dig holes into the ground like a Jack.

Fortunately, a good bathing session can be perfect for when you are trying to take care of your dog. There are several steps that you can use to make the process of bathing a Jack Russell Terrier as easy to handle as it can be.

1. Start by training the dog to come over to the bathing area. Offer a good treat when it comes to your spot for bathing. The key is to get the dog to associate the bathing spot with positive feelings.

You can always use a traditional bathtub if desired. Any spot that is safe for the Jack Russell Terrier to be in and is not really dirty or crowded will be a good place for the bath to be in. If the spot is already familiar to the dog in some way then it should be even easier to get the process taken care of the right way.

2. Make sure you are gentle with the water as you add it onto the dog's coat. Use calm water and keep it from being overly cold or hot.

One good idea is to consider having a pitcher of water to use at this point. This should be applied calmly and with just enough of a motion. This is better than just using a tap or hose and watering the dog with water whose rate of flow cannot be controlled.

3. Add shampoo from the neck down and lather it into the coat.

Make sure you use a dog-specific shampoo. A dog-specific shampoo product will be designed to fit in well with its coat and not put the dog at risk of irritation or other problems that might come about for any purpose.

4. After lathering the shampoo around, making sure that you get around as much of the hair as possible, be sure to clear it out with some more gentle water.

Make sure you do not get anything in the dog's eyes, ears or mouth. We'll talk about cleaning those parts of the body a little bit later in this guide.

5. As you dry the dog, use a comb and a heat-free hair dryer. This should make it easier for the dog's hair to become comfortable.

Never use a hair dryer for people. The heat from such a dryer will hurt the dog's coat.

This process for cleaning the dog's coat should not be all that hard to handle. You just have to use the right materials to make it easier for the dog's coat to stay clean and clear. Doing this can make a huge difference in the dog's self-esteem and will help you get closer to the dog after a while.

2) Nail Care

The process of clipping your dog's nails should not be hard to do. In fact, this might sound like something that is bothersome but the truth is that clipping one's nails on occasion is better than having the dog declawed.

If you declawed your Jack then you would pretty much have someone tearing out key bones and nerves in your dog's feet. This in turn can be painful and discouraging to the dog. Some animal rights groups have also considered this act to be outright abusive.

It's best to keep the dog's nails intact. Still, you need to trim them every week or so. This is to keep the dog from being at risk of scratching things in your home and damaging them. Also, if the dog's nails are trimmed then the dog will be less likely to feel pain while walking or running around a spot.

This is a great process to consider but you must make sure that you avoid using traditional clippers. Only use clippers that are for dog use. This is to allow the nails to be trimmed at the right spots and to actually get towards the angles that the dog's hair would be in.

The trimmers that you see above are great to have as they contain the right curves to go after the dog's nails with. This ensures that there will not be much of a risk of tugging when this is used the right way.

Here are some steps to use here:

1. First, clean off the dog-friendly nail trimmers.

2. Make sure the dog is calm as you get ready to trim its nails.

3. Place the trimmers at the end of the light spot of the nail. Specifically, you should trim the nails above their dark spots. The dark spots are where the veins for the nails are located. If you cut there then the dog might be at risk of bleeding.

4. Use a separate nail file if desired to sand down the nail after cutting it.

5. A styptic pencil may be used on the nail in the event that you accidentally cut it too low and the nail starts bleeding. This pencil can help apply a coating onto the nail that will stop the bleeding.

This is a process that should work quite well provided that you keep the dog calm. If you do it with care then the dog will feel a little more comfortable with the process. Give the dog a treat after you are done, as it will allow the dog to link the process of getting its nails trimmed with a reward for being nice when it is all being taken care of.

Additional Tips

You can use a few added tips to enhance the overall process of trimming your dog's nails:

- Make sure your dog is used to having its paws handled by someone else. Your dog needs to become used to this at an early age so the dog will feel more comfortable with the process. This is to keep your Jack from being at risk of running off right in the middle of the cutting process.

- If you are just starting to cut your dog's nails then you

might want to be gentle. You might have to cut one or two nails at a time and then move on to cutting more nails after every couple of cutting sessions.

- You should not have to go all the way down to the area right above the quick when you trim your dog's nail. It might help to trim the tip off and then the next. This two-pass process can be a necessity as a dog's nails can be much thicker than your own and will require extra care.

3) Ear Care

The large ears on the Jack Russell Terrier might look adorable but it is critical that you make sure you wash the dog's ears on occasion. This includes making sure the inside parts of the ears are taken care of. You must protect the insides of the ears or else the dog will be at risk of infections and other common problems that might come about as a result of the area being far too dirty.

Not all Jacks have ears that are perked upward but it helps to at least watch for how the ears will develop.

It is best to use cotton balls in this process. Do not use cotton swabs as they can get stuck in the dog's ear. A cotton ball will be easier to hold and much more comfortable.

Here's what you need to do:

1. Trim the hair around the dog's ear. Don't have lots of hair bits covering areas around the ears or else it will be harder for you to actually take care of the ears in a proper manner.

2. Use a dog ear rinse solution on a cotton ball. This should not contain any alcohol, antibiotics or steroids.

3. Apply the solution on the ball into the ear. Move it around the inside part of the ear so it will destroy many forms of bacteria within the ear.

4. Start working on the outside parts of the ear. Don't go any deeper than what you are comfortable with.

5. Wet a new cotton ball and use that to wash the inner ear.

This is a process that should be done once a week as a means of protecting your dog's ears.

Also, watch for how the cotton balls come out. If they appear to be really dirty then it might help to talk with your vet to see if there is a more significant problem that needs to be treated in some way.

4) Eye Care

Your dog's eyes need to be cleaned on occasion as well. You need to do this to not only ensure that your dog's vision will be protected but to also ensure that the dog will not be at risk of serious problems relating to infections around the eyes.

Here are some steps to use in order to clean the dog's eyes.

1. Like with the ears, trim hairs around the eyes to ensure that they will not cover over the eyes. Do this only when the dog is comfortable and will not feel overly agitated.

2. Use a sterile eye wash compound that you can find at a local pet supply store. Insert one or two drops into the eyes. The specific amount that you need will vary based on what the bottle you have says.

3. Use the same washing compound with a cotton ball around the hair near the eyes. This is to remove tear stains. Tear stains can build up bacteria and keep your Jack's face from looking as beautiful as it is supposed to.

Be careful when doing this so the dog will not feel irritated as you proceed. Try to possibly offer a treat when you are done so the dog will feel comfortable about what you were doing.

Be sure to also watch for the type of cleaner that you want to use. Make sure that the cleaner you have is one that is fully suitable for your dog and has the right components to make it fully functional and suitable for its needs.

Additional Pointers

The process of cleaning off your dog's eyes can double as a time period to use when trying to check and see if there are any serious problems in its eyes. There are many tips that can be used as you take care of the dog's eyes:

- Gently move the dog's lower eyelid down and check on its condition as you wash the eye. Make sure it has a pink look to it. If it has a white or red look then it means that something may be wrong with the dog's eyes.

- Check to see if the dog's pupils are of the same size on each eye. Contact your vet in the event that one pupil does not appear right.

- Make sure the dog doesn't have any discharges, crusting materials or other things around the corners of its eyes. While these might look harmless, these may be signs of serious problems with the dog's eyes.

5) Clipping

Clipping is a practice that entails trimming off excess hair bits from your dog. There are many reasons why you might clip your dog's hair:

- There are some snags in the dog's coat that need to be removed so you can actually run a comb through the hair without any problems.

- You may also need to keep excess hair from being a threat around the dog's ears and eyes.

- In some cases the hair might contain fleas or other materials that have to be kept out of the dog's coat.

Either way, clipping can help you ensure that your dog's hair will be treated the right way and that nothing wrong is going to be found within that coat. Still, you need to be careful when clipping your dog's hair. Failing to take care of it the right way can cause the coat to look uneven.

There are a few simple things that can be done now to make the clipping process easy to work with:

- Make sure you stick with scissors that are blunt and are appropriately styled. Look for scissors that are slightly curved and not sharp so they will not irritate the dog in any way. Good scissors can come with ends that have slight stoppers on them and will not be pointy and potentially harmful to anyone who uses them the wrong way.

- Choose scissors that feature blades or components that will quickly take in the hair that you have. Be sure that you keep the hair comfortable so it will not be at risk of any serious problems over time.

- Keep the dog calm at all times. Don't cut unless the dog is relaxed.

- When cutting, cut away from the coat. Make sure the hair is trimmed evenly to where the hair will not be pulled or forced in. Instead, see that the cut is done carefully and evenly.

You could potentially go for an electric razor for dogs but that is illogical for the Jack Russell Terrier. If anything, those electric razors are better suited for dogs with much longer coats than what a Jack has.

6) Dental Care

Your dog's teeth need to be treated with care. If your dog's teeth are not healthy and treated right then it will be very difficult for your dog to feel healthy. There will be a potential for gum disease and bacteria to develop around the dog's teeth if they are not treated well. Your dog's breath will be bothersome too.

Plaque and bacteria can quickly form around your dog's teeth. This will harden over time and become tartar.

This will cause problems like bad breath and gum disease. The worst part is that sometimes this tartar can cause gingivitis. The dog's teeth may also become loose while the gums will wear out. If this is not treated as soon as possible then the teeth will have to be examined and reviewed by your vet.

Dental care plans can help but it's essential to keep the teeth cleaned right with only the best materials:

1. Use a dog-based toothbrush that is double-ended and features the bristles at angles so they will actually target the dog's teeth quite well.

2. Use an appropriate dog toothpaste. **Do not use anything that contains fluoride (toothpaste for human use)** as it is poisonous to dogs.

3. Brush the teeth with a standard motion like what you would do for your own teeth.

Complete this process two to three times in a week if possible. Also, if the dog is not willing to get its teeth brushed then don't worry. You can use a short brushing session at the start and then increase the time you spend brushing its teeth over time so the dog will become used to the practice.

The timing for taking care of your dog's teeth should be kept under control. You might have to be certain that you do this for about thirty to sixty seconds at a time. This should be enough to give your teeth the help that they deserve.

There are many other things to do with regards to taking care of your dog's teeth:

- Use dry food in your dog's diet as it will not stick to the dog's teeth.

- Offer chew toys and bones that can help support proper dental health and potentially keep plaque from developing.

- Watch for the colours in your dog's teeth. If they start to become unusual in appearance then take your dog to the vet to see if there is some kind of underlying issue involved with the teeth.

One intriguing option to have is a brush that fits over your finger.

This might create a good sense of control that you can use to keep the brushing process under control without being any harder to handle than needed.

7) Skin Care

Your dog's skin needs to be treated with care. This is especially important for the Jack Russell Terrier whose coat may not be as long as you might expect it to be.

Your dog's skin has to be treated with care by ensuring the dog will not have any itchy spots, rashes or other areas that the dog might scratch or chew on often. It might be easy for the dog to develop bacteria in some of these spots that it chews and scratches around.

There are several things that you can do with regards to your dog's skin care needs:

- Watch for any redness or tender spots around the dog's skin. You can find these while bathing the dog.

- Keep your home humidified so the dog's skin will not dry up.

- If the dog is to go outside in cold conditions then provide your dog with a little cover around its body. It does not have to be overly elaborate; it just has to be something that can create a slight barrier of protection between the dog and any cold conditions that are outside.

- Brush your pet often so you will stimulate the blood vessels around the skin. This should help encourage the dog's skin to feel healthier and a little more vibrant.

- A good moisturizer can be used on your dog's skin if needed. Stick with a healthy moisturizer that is formulated for your dog's skin though.

- Always check the paw pads on your dog after it goes outside or for a walk. This is to see if there are any cuts or other things that might be found on its paw pads. You can use a proper patching cream to heal these problems on the pads if you ever see anything wrong with them.

Remember that the dog's coat has to be treated the right way to ensure that it will stay healthy. You must be careful so you know that you will have more control over your dog's appearance while giving off a better look to its coat.

8) Brushing and Combing

It's always enjoyable to have a brush and comb that you can use on your Jack. After all, a good weekly opportunity to brush and comb your dog's coat will give you time to spend with your dog.

More importantly, it helps to get rid of dead hair bits. The thing is that the Jack can shed just like any other dog breed. The last thing you need is loads of hair all over your house.

A brushing plan can be used to gather up old hair bits and get rid of them. This in turn will make your dog look beautiful and feel happier because there is not going to be too much pressure building up around its skin.

In addition, brushing helps you to keep the coat smooth and clean. You can also identify snags in the hair where the hair appears to be stuck together.

If you're going to brush or comb the dog's coat then you should be doing so once or twice in a week to keep the dog's coat healthy. Also, the brushing should be done in a gentle motion that goes alongside the flow of the dog's hair.

This in turn should create a good feeling in the dog's coat and will make the dog feel more comfortable about what you are doing.

You should make sure that you clean out your brush after each use though. You do not want the dog's hair to build up and clump itself together into the comb you have. Make sure the comb is fully cleaned out as you are done using so it will be ready for use the next time you need to clean something out.

There are many additional tips to use while taking care of your dog's coat:

- Make sure you do this before bathing, as tangles are harder to remove if they are wet.

- If a matted part of the coat is not coming out then feel free to trim it.

- Don't get the brush onto the skin as it may irritate the dog if it gets to be far too close.

A smooth comb can be used to straighten the dog's hair after you are done brushing old hair out of it. This will create one final look of elegance and beauty in the dog's hair when you do it right.

After this is done, a separate comb will have to be used.

A comb will clearly be slimmer than that of something else you might use. Still, it can be perfect if you want to keep your dog's coat looking great. Make sure you use it after brushing so it will not pick up loads of hair.

Chapter 9: Daily Feeding and Care

Every dog needs to have a good amount of food in order to stay healthy and happy. This can be a challenge for some to handle but if you understand what you have to do with it then it should be relatively easy for you to get the most out of your dog's health.

You must measure the dog's diet carefully. You will have to watch for how you're feeding your dog as failing to feed your dog the right way can result in serious health issues over an extended period of time.

The amount of food that a Jack Russell Terrier requires obviously is not as great as what you might expect to get out of a much larger breed. Still, you will have to feed it quite a bit in order for that dog to say healthy and happy.

The plans that you will use for feeding and caring for your Jack can make a huge difference. Let's talk about this for a good bit.

This chapter will also discuss many points relating to the daily forms of care that you will use. You have to be careful with regards to how you will be taking care of your dog so you know that it will get into a healthy routine and become more likely to stay fit for as long as it potentially can.

1) The Type of Food

The type of food that you will be serving to your Jack should be prepared with care. The food must include the following:

- Proteins that come from lean meat and fish; do not use any animal by-products

- Healthy carbohydrates; plants and grains are also important to have in one's food

- A lack of fillers; be sure to especially avoid wheat and corn

- Vitamins and minerals

In addition, you should try and use at least 75 percent dry kibble in your dog's diet. This will encourage healthy teeth and gums. This is because the dog will not be at risk of developing lots of plaque and bacteria around its teeth and gums if it consumes only the healthiest type of food that it will not struggle to consume.

Be sure to talk with your veterinarian about the options that your Jack can use. Also, try and keep the food that is being served as consistent as possible. If you are unable to do this then the dog will start to become overly selective.

2) Feeding Meat

Your dog will need meat in order to survive. Meat products will contain the necessary proteins that a dog needs in order to stay healthy.

It is true that many dog food products are made with an assortment of meat items. However, you can always feed your dog plenty of straight meats just as well.

Meats can be ideal as they can help you balance your dog's diet. You will have more protein and fat in the meat plus fewer carbohydrates when compared with what you'd get out of a dry dog food product.

Your dog's body will have a much easier time digesting its foods while having a healthier coat, a better stool and an improved potential to control one's weight without being any harder to manage than what is necessary.

In fact, raw meats will be safe for your dog to consume. You don't even have to do anything special to prepare meat for your dog to have.

You need to use a few points before choosing to feed your dog any kind of meat:

- Be sure that the meet you serve is as safe as possible. While you can serve your dog raw meat, it helps to see that the meat is not discolored, bruised or otherwise unsightly in its appearance.

- Trim off any fatty spots on the meat before serving. These fatty spots are often filled with excess calories that will do nothing.

- Avoid anything that has been heavily processed. These processed items tend to contain far too many by-products and fillers just to make the meats look good or taste like they do.

- Make sure the straightforward meats that you serve consist of about 25 percent or so of your dog's diet on average.

This is a great solution for your dog's diet but it helps for you to take a careful look at the way your dog's meats are prepared. Be sure you stick with safe and sensible meats for your dog to have. Always be certain that you have meats that are fresh and easy to consume.

Most importantly, don't ever play around with unusual cooking methods for your dog's meat. Many traditional procedures for cooking meat can create issues that may be harmful to your dog. This can come from dangerous enzymes that may be generated or additives that can go into the meat during the cooking process. Sticking with raw meats will clearly be the best way to go.

What About Bacteria?

Your dog's digestive system is shorter than yours and is much more acidic than what you have. Therefore, your dog will not be at as much of a risk to develop problems from a bacterial infection that is caused by meat. These include infections from the salmonella and E. coli bacteria.

Still, you must be careful when preparing any meats for your dog. Make sure the meats are clean and safe to serve before giving them to your dog.

Is a Vegan Diet Healthy?

Contrary to what you might think, a vegan diet is not going to be any good to a dog as it could be to a regular person. Your dog's body is more dependent on protein than yours. As a result, a vegan diet could end up being very harmful to your dog's body.

This might not sound all that appealing if you are on a vegan diet yourself or you are trying to avoid meats for some particular purpose. Still, you must be careful with regards to what your dog is going to consume. If your dog consumes lots of protein then it will stay healthy. If your dog doesn't consume any meat then it will be at risk of serious harm and will not stay healthy.

3) Feeding Puppies

You have to be aware of how you will be feeding any puppy terrier. The thing about daily feeding procedures is that the puppy needs to have plenty of food in order to grow properly.

Naturally, the mother will provide the puppy with much of its diet at the start of its life. After that, you will have to offer several different types of materials for your dog's needs.

A puppy will need about 800 to 1000 calories of food in a day. This should be good for its overall health by ensuring that it will grow as needed.

It will help to get about 1.25 of 1.75 cups of food each day. This should be divided up in two or three meals over the course of the day. Be consistent as to when you will be feeding your Jack.

4) Feeding Adults

You will also have to feed your adult Jack 1.25 to 1.75 cups of food in a day. However, the food that you will serve needs to have fewer calories. An adult Jack can have about 400 to 700 calories in a day in order to keep one's body sturdy.

The 1.25-1.75 cup standard is important as the Jack is not able to eat far too much food in a typical day. Don't feed the dog anything more than needed or else the dog might be at risk of struggling with weight gain. Also, a dog might vomit out one's food if it has far too much in one day.

Be sure to watch for your Jack's rate of growth. Always adjust your Jack's diet based on what is consumes and watch for how it responds to the diet that you feed it. Be certain that the diet you are preparing for your dog is sensible and healthy at all times so it will not be at risk of harm and that it will actually get the amount of food that it really needs.

5) Notes About Treats

We've talked about treats in the process of training your dog (and we'll talk a little more about it in an upcoming chapter) but we need to be specific with regards to how treats are to be used. Naturally, treats are used as a means of rewarding your dog and making it happy.

However, you need to be fully aware of what you're going to get out of your treats. You have to see that you are giving treats only at the right times. Specifically, you must only do this when the dog is behaving properly.

Now, treats can be found in a variety of great options. These include plenty of foods with delicious meat flavors that dogs often crave.

However, you have to be very careful when finding these dog treats. There are many critical things to be aware of:

- Avoid treats that are made from outside the country.

- Fresh human foods like berries, frozen peas, raw almonds or small strips of organic lean meat may be offered. This is provided that the foods are healthy and not part of a listing of foods for the dog to avoid (which will be discussed in a moment).

- Make sure you stick with only a few treats at a particular time. In fact, treats should only make for up to 10 percent of your dog's daily diet.

- Check on the contents of the treats. Make sure the first ingredients are actually worthwhile and don't contain fillers, by-products and other items. Also, avoid having anything that is overly dangerous or harmful in your dog's diet.

Be careful as you get your dog's treats ready so you will not be putting your dog in any trouble. You should make sure that you stick with only the right options.

6) What Dog Treats Work Best?

Now you might find lots of different treats on the market with many of them being packaged in all sorts of forms. However, you have to stick only with foods that you know will be healthy for the dog to consume.

The problem with so many dog treats is that they are made with random things that can be harmful to the dog's body if not taken care of the right way. Besides, you might find natural dog treats like what you'll read about in a bit to be a little more affordable in comparison.

Let's take a look at a few options for what dog treats can work well for your loved one's diet:

- Green beans
- Baby carrots
- Broccoli
- Banana slices
- Berries
- Watermelon bits
- Apple slices (cored)
- Plain rice cakes (break them down first)

These are healthy and contain plenty of smart nutrients and will be easy for the dog to digest. They will not contain far too many calories either.

More importantly, they are not dangerous like the foods that we are going to be talking about in a moment.

The treats that you can safely feed can go alongside many other healthy treats that your dog can enjoy. These include such popular treats as traditional bone-shaped snacks.

7) Foods To Avoid

While your dog might be turned on by the scents of certain foods in your home, they may also be foods that are very dangerous for it to have. You must make sure you avoid feeding your dog the following foods as they will cause some serious threats to your dog if they are used:

Chocolate

Chocolate contains caffeine and theobromine, two components that are harmful to dogs. These can cause vomiting and irregular heart actions.

Milk, Cheese and Other Dairy Products

Milk that you can get from a typical store contains sugars that the dog is unable to break down. It is very different from the milk that its mother produces. The same goes for other daily-related products like cheese. These can cause diarrhea and vomiting.

Onions and Garlic

Onions can cause serious damages to a dog's red blood cells. It makes it harder for the cells to develop and form. This can cause the dog to become weak.

Garlic can especially be a threat. This can clearly cause red blood cells around the body to weaken and be at risk of serious harm.

Macadamia Nuts

Although some other nuts like what were listed earlier can be healthy, macadamia nuts are dangerous to dogs. Research is needed to determine why they are dangerous but it is known that a dog who consumes them can develop issues relating to vomiting, depression and tremors in one's body.

Grapes and Raisins

It is uncertain as to why grapes and raisins are toxic to dogs. However, they are known to cause the kidneys to fail rather quickly.

Avocados

Persin, a toxin inside the avocado, is dangerous to dogs. It can cause an upset stomach and breathing problems that can be very serious if not treated right.

Apple Cores

While the outside parts of an apple should be safe to a dog, the core is dangerous as it contains cyanide. Traces of cyanide are capable of doing damage to any dog's body. If you are going to feed a dog any apple-related items then you need to be certain that the core is completely removed.

Bacon

Bacon can cause pancreatitis in your dog's body. This can cause serious digestive problems.

Caffeine

Caffeine contains methylated xanthine, a compound that can cause vomiting and other serious problems.

An interesting point of note about this listing is that there are many companies that sell milk products for dogs. These are products that have been formulated to be safe for dogs to have. If you ever hear stories about "milk for dogs" or "(insert other food that is normally supposed to be banned here) for dogs" then please talk with your vet about so you can get more information on if this is actually right for your dog to have.

8) Ingredients In Dog Food To Avoid

While many dog food companies insist on making sure that their products are safe and healthy for your dog, there are still some ingredients in their products that might actually be harmful to your dog. They are not dangerous and threatening, however, they are problematic ingredients that need to be avoided.

These are ingredients that are often thrown into different foods as a means of cutting all kinds of costs. These choices need to be explored carefully.

Here are a few of the many different ingredients that you have to avoid when it comes to finding dog food.

Grains

The digestive tract of a dog, especially a smaller dog like a Jack, is not as strong as what people have. As a result, it is often hard for the dog to digest the grains that it might consume.

In fact, the digestive tract is designed to digest meat above anything else. Therefore, it is important to avoid any direct grains like corn, soybeans or other commonplace ingredients. These are dangerous ingredients that can be harmful to your dog's body due to its inability to process it as well.

Of course, many different dog foods will contain items that are based off of many grains. You must be certain when finding such foods that you don't stick with ones that are far too filled with dangerous fillers.

Direct Meat Slices

It's clear that dogs can have meats from many outside sources. You can always give your dog plenty of fine lean means that are capable of giving it the protein that the body requires.

But what about the meats that come in the dog food products you see on the market right now? These include many of the meats that come in different canned wet food products.

Meats that are already slices and prepared in sauces and other materials for your dog to consume should sound great in theory. They are fully canned and ready to serve to your dog.

However, these meats may actually be dangerous for many reasons:

- They often come from animals that are diseased or dying, if not actually dead.

- They are often from meat sources that are prepared with hormones and antibiotics. These are ingredients that are often dangerous to meat sources as they can cause the natural components in meat to wear out.

- Some of these meats actually come from different by-product sources. These include the many parts of an animal that we people would not eat ourselves.

These meats are often treated this way as a means of keeping the cost of handling such meats down. It's all about making a profit and it is being done at the expense of the welfare of your Jack.

Therefore, if you are going to feed your Jack any straightforward meat (which you should) then you should only stick with actual meat sources like what you can find at a typical grocery store. This will be a safer option for you to have.

Animal Digest

Animal digest is a commonly-listed ingredient in many dog food products. This is a component that is made out of boiled renderings that come from animals. That is, the meat that comes from an animal's body will be boiled to ensure that its bacteria is removed and could technically be safe to eat.

The worst part of animal digest is that it can come from many sources:

- Assorted cattle; these include cattle that did not meet certain standards to be prepared as traditional meat products
- Roadkill found on highways
- Stray animals that are picked up and killed off
- Animals that are euthanized at some shelters
- Even some older domesticated animals that had to be put down could be included

This is all done just to try and make sure more meat can come out of animals that might not have been suitable for the process. It is a crude and difficult procedure that may actually do more harm than help.

In fact, animal digest has been known to contain traces of components that are used in the euthanasia process. These traces are not deadly but it does make for an extremely legitimate concern. Do you really want your healthy Jack to actually consume something that is supposed to kill a dog?

Be sure to avoid any foods that contain this animal digest. You never know where it's going to come from.

Greasy Fat Materials

If you open up a bag of dog food and you start to sense some funny greasy smell coming out of it then that means the dog food has been coated with greasy fat materials. These are often added as a means of creating a scent that will entice the dog into actually eating the food.

This is a recognizable scent that the dog will certainly enjoy. In addition, the dog will feel extra motivated to go forward and consume the food. However, there is a huge problem in that this will add more fat than what's necessary to the food.

Sure, your dog needs plenty of fat in order to stay healthy and to have a comfortable coat and body. However, if you give your dog too much fat then it will be at risk of becoming overweight.

Besides, the greasy fat stuff that is added to the food is not actually going to do a thing to the food. It is practically an empty additive. Therefore, you should avoid this part of the food.

Assorted Preservatives

Preservatives are often added to many dog foods to make them capable of lasting as long as possible. That is, they will have longer shelf lives.

However, the preservatives like BHT, BHA and ethoxyquin that can be found in some foods can be especially dangerous:

- Preservatives can often cause the digestive system to wear out over time.

- The liver and kidneys will stop functioning properly after a while if the dog has too many preservatives.

- Some components may be linked to certain cancers, particularly stomach cancer.

- Many of these preservatives are not even designed with

food purposes in mind. For instance, ethoxyquin is a Monsanto-made product that helps preserve rubber surfaces and components.

The biggest problem with these preservatives is that they may be in your dog's food. This is especially the case in the United States. There are more laws in Europe with regards to keeping preservatives out of dog food than what there are in other parts of the world.

Be careful when reviewing the ingredients in your dog's food and make sure it doesn't have any preservatives. In fact, this point leads to the last topic of discussion in this section.

Anything That Just Sounds Unusual

Of course, any kind of food out there is going to contain a full listing of its ingredients. You need to be more careful with these listings when finding foods for your Jack than anything else.

This is all down to the dog not having as strong of a digestive system as you might think. Sure, it may not be at risk of bacterial issues all the time, but it is still going to be unable to process some ingredients.

Simply put, if you ever seen anything in your dog's food that looks or sounds unusual then it is best for you to avoid serving it altogether. Don't ever give your dog anything that looks outright unusual or strange or else your dog will be at risk of serious harm.

9) Exercise

Everyone needs a bit of exercise in their lives. The odds are you could use some exercise just as well. However, it is always important for a small dog like a Jack to get the exercise that it demands so it can stay healthy.

Exercise is important as your Jack Russell Terrier needs to be active and healthy. As one of the most energetic dogs in the world it should not be too hard to find your Jack being active and ready.

Your plans for exercise with your dog should be prepared with plenty of ideas relating to keeping your dog ready for whatever might come about. You need to make sure you get your dog ready for all the activities that you want to get into so your dog will feel happy and healthy.

It's best to give your dog about 30 to 45 minutes of exercise each day. This is a good timeframe for keeping your dog healthy.

Exercise can work quite well for your dog's needs. Here's a good look at what you can get when it comes to keeping your dog healthy:

- You will have to walk your dog on occasion. This will be discussed a little later on in this chapter.

- Make sure you start giving your dog exercise with fetching activities on occasion. Teach your dog to go after something and then come back to you.

- Frisbee throwing and retrieval can be a great thing to explore just as well.

- You can bring your dog to a dog park in the region to allow your dog to play with other dogs and get to know them while also running around and getting more than enough exercise over time. This can make for an exciting time that allows people to get in touch with each other.

10) Playtime Ideas

The playtime plans that you get into with your Jack Russell Terrier can be fun for all to see. You might want to think about some playtime options that especially target the active nature of the Jack. Here's a look at the way the playtime activities with your dog can be utilized in order to keep your dog active:

- Tug-of-war is an activity that allows you to not only give your dog exercise by biting on something and dragging it from you but will also encourage lessons on how to listen to you while that dog is excited.

- Fetching, as mentioned earlier, can be healthy and fun to do.

- You can play a chasing activity where you are running with a toy on a string and the Jack has to catch it. This will give you and the dog some exercise.

- Hide and seek can be enjoyable as you can call the dog over when you get to a certain spot to see if the dog can find this. This can help the dog to associate a certain sound with you so that dog will know to come around the area when you make that signal.

You should certainly schedule some playtime to go within the activities that your dog will get into. If you are capable of engaging in playtime then your dog will feel happy and will want to get a good workout with you.

11) Walking

Dog walking is a time-honored tradition. It's an activity that is important as your dog will receive the exercise it needs while you will get the dog's energy to be properly exerted.

Dog walking is great but you should use a few standards:

- Keep a walk about 20 to 45 minutes in length so the dog will not become overly tired midway through.

- Keep the lead when walking. Walk in front of the dog so you will assert yourself as the leader of the pack.

- Use a short leash when walking. This is to give you more control.

- Provide the food and water that your dog wants to it after the walk is over. Consider this to be a good reward.

- Don't be too rough or hard on the dog while walking. Make sure the dog is kept happy and don't tug on the dog; make sure the dog moves with you without being forced.

What About With Other Dogs?

A dog like a Jack can be walked with many others dogs. However, it is important to ensure that the dogs are all familiar with one another. You need to allow the dogs to get in touch with each other and to see that they are not going to be a problem to anyone.

Also, keep the dogs about one or two feet from each other. Make sure they have their own spaces.

You also need to start moving forward at the start. This is to let the dogs know that you are the one that will be in charge of getting someone to move forward.

12) While You Are Away

It's clear that you cannot stay at home with your Jack all day long. However, you need to be careful when it comes to keeping your dog alone at home.

You don't have to think that your dog is going to place your home in jeopardy while you are out. There are many things that you can do in order to keep your dog from being irritated in some way:

- Give your dog the biggest meal of the day before you leave. This is to ensure that the dog will be more likely to sleep while you are out.

- Give your dog the exercise that they need so the Jack will feel happy and comfortable while not having a potential to exert one's energy all over the house while you are out.

- Offer some good toys to have around the house. Fill them with safe and healthy treats if possible. Anything that keeps the dog occupied will help.

- You might even noticed that some television and video programs may offer soothing sounds and visuals for dogs to see. This might be an interesting thing to spot but you should be careful with regards to how these work. The problem with some video programs is that they might not work with some dogs.

Don't expect your dog to definitely watch TV while you are out but it helps to be aware of what you can do for your dog to ensure that it will not be at risk of getting in trouble while you are gone.

13) Traveling

If you plan on traveling to and from different spots then you will need to be fully aware of what you are getting into out here. You must be careful when traveling with your Jack Russell Terrier as the dog might become overly excited at times.

It's not hard to make your dog feel comfortable while you travel around to different spots. Here are a few smart ideas for you to think about when it comes to bringing your Jack to different places:

- Make sure you exercise your dog before packing your friend into a proper crate.

- Make sure you also crate train your dog so he or she will be more comfortable in the crate (refer to the earlier chapter on this).

- Make sure the dog and the crate are properly restrained. Don't ever let the dog roam around in a car or other thing while being transported.

- Allow your dog to relieve itself before traveling. This is to reduce the potential for the dog to have some kind of accident while traveling.

- Bring a good toy with your dog so the dog will have something to play with.

- Whatever you do, don't ever use any sedatives or other medications to calm your dog down before traveling. Those will only harm the dog and potentially cause a dependency of sorts.

- If driving, be sure to stop and pull over your vehicle every two to three hours to allow the dog to relieve itself or to play among other things. This is to make the dog feel comfortable and to get its energy out. Fortunately, there are plenty of open parks, rest areas and other spots that you can take your dog out to for this purpose.

- If flying, see what the policy for taking your dog on board is. Some airlines will let you take a dog on board but in most cases you might need to allow someone to watch over your dog in a separate spot on the plane. This is especially important if you're going to be on a flight that will take a while.

- If you are going to stay in a hotel then make sure you check and see if that hotel is a pet-friendly one. Be aware that some hotels may also charge extra for having pets in their rooms.

Be sure that you are fully prepared when you are trying to get your dog to travel with you quite well. Your Jack Russell Terrier will certainly be happy to be around you if you just use these pointers.

Chapter 10: Socialising

Every dog can be social. In fact, the overall process of socialization will not be all that hard for you to handle as long as you keep your dog happy.

You can use plenty of sensible socialisation plans for your Jack Russell Terrier to make it happy. However, you need to make sure they start as soon as possible.

It is best to get your dog socialized at about 8 to 12 weeks of age. However, socialisation can take place at any later point in the dog's life. Still, you must socialise the dog as early as possible in its life as it might be easier for the dog to respond properly when it is easier to influence.

It is much easier for the dog to become familiar with people and to feel comfortable around them when these points are used.

1) With Dogs and Other Pets

You should be careful when trying to get your Jack Russell Terrier to interact with other dogs. Specifically, you need to be certain that your dog is in constant interaction with other dogs and pets at a young age. This is to ensure that the Jack will be comfortable with all the other pets that it might come across over time.

There's no telling what dogs you might come across when taking your Jack to different places.

Socialisation can be done through plenty of activities:

- Playing at dog parks
- Being brought to different group dog walking activities
- Hanging around neighboring dogs in your area
- Gradually meeting other dogs while one is being cared for

In some cases you might find that your dog might be socialised through the assistance of the kennel or breeder that you took the dog in from. You might want to ask the place of interest to you if it has worked in some way to ensure that the dog is appropriately socialised.

Be sure that your dog is actually getting along with the others that it is trying to be social with. Don't assume that the dog is going to just be friendly with other dogs for the sake of doing so. Your dog needs to have a good connection with others.

2) With Other People

Again, you need to ensure that the dog is in contact with other people at an early age. As mentioned earlier, dogs tend to be trusting of others if they know that they are kept comfortable in the right spots.

Many things can be done to socialise your puppy:

- Train your puppy to learn new commands and actions.

- Keep a healthy bond with your puppy. Make sure you are kind and don't ignore what it wants from you.

- Keep tabs on the many routines that your dog is getting into.

- Bring your Jack with you on short trips if desired. These include trips to and from different places around town (provided that those places will allow you to bring a dog with you).

- Allow your dog to play with toys with you. Show that you are a trustworthy play partner.

Be sure that your dog is ready for socialisation with other people as well. Allow the dog to have a bit of time to take a look around a local spot and see who is there. Don't be afraid if the Jack starts to sniff other people; the odds are the dog is looking to see who in an area may be safe.

3) Careful Treatment

The most important thing to do with regards to socialising is to see that your dog is being treated the right way. You must be certain that the dog doesn't get agitated.

Don't be physically tough on the Jack. Its small body can be fragile and easily influenced.

Also, if the Jack seems to be struggling for any purpose, particularly when it is being held, then feel free to let it go for a moment. The dog may either have a little too much energy or it might not be willing to be handled too much at a given time. If you hold onto the dog for far too long then it might become aggravated and tough to bear with.

Most importantly, if your dog is tired or fatigued then don't try to force it into doing anything more than what it has already been doing.

Be cautious with your Jack Russell Terrier and it will feel happy and be more likely to want to stick around with you for a while. Don't ever be harder than needed and make sure the dog is happy around other pets so it will stay comfortable.

Chapter 11: Training

Dog training is not something that many people look forward to. It's a process that can take a while and not all dogs are willing to go along with it.

However, dog training can make a world of difference to any dog. Training is done to ensure that your dog will know what it is supposed to do around you.

In fact, you work with an extended variety of different training exercises with your dog. From basic commands to simply teaching interesting and fun tricks, there are many great things that you can do with your dog to make it happy to be around you and to obey you.

One of the most popular aspects of the Jack Russell Terrier is that it is a breed that is rather easy to train. In particular, it will not be all that hard for the breed to feel comfortable with you if you just know what you are going to do with it.

You need to train your dog to ensure that it will feel comfortable around you and also so it will not get into any kind of trouble with you. If you just work hard enough to get your dog trained the right way then it will be very easy for you to keep your dog happy and ready for whatever you want out of it.

Still, you have to be certain that you're going to watch over your dog and how it will behave. Your dog can be important to you but you need to ensure that whatever you are doing is something that is comfortable and easy for the dog to handle.

A Quick Note

Remember to make sure the training process works after the dog has received its exercise or has used the bathroom among other things. While any time can be a good time to train your dog, you need to do this when the Jack is actually focused.

If the dog is hungry, wound up or really has to use the bathroom then it will not be all that focused on you. It's up to you to make sure you take your dog and make sure it actually takes care of whatever business it has before beginning any kind of training process. You must be certain that your dog is ready to do whatever before anything can come about.

1) Choosing a Disciplinary Sound

You will clearly have to make sure you express a certain disciplinary sound if you're going to train your dog. This might sound unusual for the first thing to discuss in the training process but it really means a lot.

It might help to have a dog whistle with you if you're going to train your dog. This is a whistle that will create a sound that dogs can hear but not people as it comes in a unique range.

This may be used in the training process as a means of making sure that your dog will respond to you and know when something is wrong. The sound that will be added may not be all that pleasing to the dog.

This can be useful but it's important to make sure you don't go overboard with whatever you are using. You have to be certain that whatever you have is maintained the right way and is not too hard to use.

Also, try to make that sound something that can be easy for anyone to repeat. While your voice will certainly be easier for the dog to recognize, you need to be careful when using it in some way.

2) Beginner Leash Session

The first thing that you can teach your Jack Russell Terrier is how to handle a leash. Specifically, you need to teach your dog how to get on a leash and use it. Leash training will allow you to help your dog learn about what is right and wrong.

This works with some simple steps:

1. Place the leash around the dog's collar.
2. Encourage the dog to move along with the leash through

the use of a treat. That is, you might want to have the treat far from the dog's reach so the dog will place some kind of effort to move.

3. Use a gentle motion when trying to keep the dog restrained. A light tug of the leash may be used in this case. Don't be aggressive; just let the dog know that it has to be careful when moving around with a leash.

4. Walk in front of the dog at all times when holding the leash. This is to show that you are in control and that the dog will have to follow you at all times.

Make sure you are careful with the leash. The dog must be comfortable and ready to handle the leash without feeling irritated while using it.

3) Basic First Commands

Let's talk about the many commands that you can use for your dog right now. These are basic commands but they can mean so much when it comes to having your Jack Russell Terrier around in your life.

It is best to use these commands several times to make it easier for you to get a dog to hear you and associate certain commands with the words or actions you use. Don't forget to get plenty of treats to encourage your dog to follow through with all of the different commands that you might teach it.

Come

Teaching a dog to come will ensure that the dog knows when to come over to you.

1. Call the dog's name or use some other sound that the dog will associate with one's name.

2. Turn and run a few steps.

3. After this, call the dog again and see if the dog will come over to you.

4. If the dog does come to you from a distance then give

your dog a treat.

Make sure you use this as often as needed. You need to make sure the dog will know when to come over to you.

Sit

The act of sitting is needed to ensure that the dog will stop in its tracks and sit down as demanded. This can be critical if the dog becomes excited over something it sees.

1. Say "sit" while bringing an empty hand onto the dog's nose. Hold your fingers out as if you were going to offer a treat.

2. Say "sit" as needed to encourage the dog to sit down. Keep this up until the dog actually sits.

3. When the dog does actually sit, praise the dog and give the dog a treat from your other hand or your pocket.

4. Try this again at another time and see if there is any form of improvement coming out of the dog's behavior. The goal is to see that the dog will link the word "sit" to the act of sitting down.

If you teach your dog to sit properly then it will not be at risk of being overly agitated or excited for any purpose. Be careful with this so the dog will feel comfortable.

Stay

If you teach your dog to stay then the dog will not move forward and will stop in its tracks. This can be important if the dog might be running off in some way or is disruptive in any manner.

1. Call your dog and tell it to come to a certain spot like a mat or bed.

2. Tell your dog to sit. (Of course, this lesson comes after the come and sit lessons.)

3. Use the "stay" command and use a good hand motion.

4. Walk backwards from the dog while continuing to use that hand motion.

5. If the dog does not listen and gets up then go back to the original location and start over.

6. If the dog stays in the same location for a given period of time then tell it to come to you.

7. Offer a treat as praise.

8. Teach this again at a later time but expand the period of time that the dog needs to stay at. Specifically, you should have the dog stay for a few extra seconds each time. This is to ensure that the dog will actually stay as demanded. Be sure to even walk to a spot where the dog will not immediately see you without placing some kind of effort to actually find you.

Heel

Teaching the dog to heel is important as it ensures that the dog will follow by you and stay close to you. That is, it is not going to think that you are trying to give up any form of command to your dog.

In particular, this is to keep the dog from pulling on the leash as you walk it. This is to show that you are in charge. It is also to keep the dog from being at risk of potentially hurting itself any further.

The process of teaching the dog to heel doesn't have to be all that hard to do either. Here are some steps that can be used to get your dog to pay attention and heel as demanded.

1. Walk with the dog on your left and the leash across from you while holding it in your right hand.

2. Have the dog walk with you with its head or shoulder even with your hip.

3. Get the dog's attention at this point. You can call the dog's name or tap its head as required.

4. Say something like "heel" as a command to get the dog to stick with you at a certain spot. Reward the dog once it gets to the particular spot that you want it to be at.

If the dog can heel then it will not be at risk of straying off from you and getting in any trouble. You can use this process to protect the dog and keep it from being at risk of harm in any form while you are walking it.

Down

As friendly as the Jack may be, it can get excited to the point where it can be restless and will jump up on someone who comes around you. This can especially be a problem if it's to someone who isn't familiar with the dog.

You will need to teach your Jack how to stay down and to get off of something or someone in the event that it is overly excited. There are a few things that can be done to make this possible and easy to handle.

1. Get the dog to sit.

2. Say the word "down" and then place a treat at the dog's nose. After this, move the treat down to the floor. Start moving the treat away from the dog like you were creating a line on the floor.

3. Ease the dog into the down position. A small push can be used if the dog needs a bit of assistance.

4. Praise the dog when it gets all the way down to the ground. You can give the dog a treat at this point.

5. Teach this regularly with the goal of getting the dog to associate this command with knowing to get down without having to physically push the dog into getting to this position.

4) Hand Signals

Hand signals may be used to teach your dog to come to you, sit or do other things. These signals can take a little longer to teach but they may be done after you teach your dog the basic commands that it should use. It's all to give your dog a visual cue for what to do in order to receive some reward or take part in some action that you want out of it.

More importantly, these hand signals can make sure there's a universal sense of control that can go about when telling your Jack to do certain things. Remember, it might be easier for a Jack (or any other dog breed for that matter) to listen to the master's voice than anyone else's.

Here are some steps to use in order to teach hand signals to your dog:

1. Use a mix of both verbal cues and hand signals that will match up with whatever you want to say to the dog. Keep them as consistent as possible so the dog will know what you want to say and do at a given time.

2. Make sure the dog understands the verbal command as you start to add the hand signals to the process.

3. Put the dog in certain situations where training is used and then use certain hand signals that are based on the commands you want but without any verbal statements. Make sure you have plenty of treats for rewarding the dog when it does things the right way.

There are many good hand signals that you can use in the process of getting a Jack Russell Terrier to learn what you want it to do:

- Stay – Hold a hand with the palm outward to suggest that it needs to stop moving.

- Come – Hold your hand outward like you are going to shake someone.

- Heel – Point your finger towards the ground.

- Sit – You can hold your hand flat and parallel to the ground and have it lower slowly to signal that you want the dog to stay.

- Down – The same motion that you used when telling your dog to sit can also be used if desired.

5) Fun Tricks

While teaching your Jack Russell Terrier about the basic

commands that it needs to follow can be important, you can also teach your Jack some interesting tricks that can be fun to show off to anyone. Here's a look at how you can do a few of these fun moves with your dog.

Shake Paws

You can teach a dog to shake paws by having it come put its paw out to you.

1. Make sure the dog is in a sitting position.

2. Hold a treat and then show it to the dog.

3. Close your hand over the treat and then hold it close to the dog's foot.

4. See that the dog lifts its paw up even if it is by a small bit. Give the dog the treat if it obeys you.

5. Test this again, making sure the dog goes a little higher up to get the treat the next time around.

6. Keep doing this until you get to the point that the initial position of your hand will be the spot that the dog will reach after.

This is a fun practice that can be attractive for many owners to try. Give it a shot when teaching your dog tricks.

Roll Over

Rolling over is a fun trick for a dog to do.

1. Kneel down and tell your down to get down as well.

2. Hold a treat to its nose with the palm upward.

3. Roll your hand to where the palm is facing down.

4. Arch your arm over the dog's head to encourage to dog to roll over.

5. Keep moving your hand to encourage the dog to roll over.

6. Give the dog the treat when it has been successfully done.

7. Make sure you also add a "roll over" command as you

continue teaching this lesson to the dog.

6) Surviving the Energy

Your Jack Russell Terrier is an energetic dog; there is no denying that. However, you need to understand that with this energy comes the potential for the dog to not pay much attention to you. It is up to you to ensure that you are keeping track of what the dog is doing and that you be patient.

More importantly, you have to be consistent and regular with your dog. You have to stay consistent to reinforce the things that you want to teach while also keeping the dog from feeling confused in some way.

You have to be certain when teaching your dog that you are careful when doing so. Don't ever mix up your commands and keep everything organized.

In fact, you might have an easier time with training your dog after it goes to the bathroom or engages in a bit of a play session. You want to make sure your dog isn't overly wound up and that it is ready to be with you at only the right time. Don't ever struggle to try and keep the dog relaxed because that dog might end up only doing things based on when you want to do something.

Most importantly, you must make sure that you never give up no matter how tough it might be for you to train your dog. Sure, it might be a challenge to get the dog to pay attention but if you just stay steady then it should be very easy for you to train your dog.

7) Obedience Classes

Some places will offer obedience classes for your Jack Russell Terrier to take part in. These are classes that will teach the dog about proper behavior through professionals who are capable of interacting with dogs.

In particular, these obedience classes are often used as a means of correcting negative or harmful behaviors that a dog might engage in. A dog can be taught to avoid begging, pulling, chewing or other things over time.

This can be great to consider as your dog will learn proper lessons on how to behave in any situation and will become a true angel when it goes through all the right lessons.

Still, as great as this can be, you need to be careful when it comes to offering obedience classes to your dog. You have to particularly watch for many important aspects of obedience classes.

Specifically, some obedience classes might take place in group settings where a dog can become easily distracted. Also, the dog might not respond well to an unfamiliar environment or to someone that the dog is not familiar with.

More importantly, you need to actually exert your own person sense of control. Some trainers are willing to help you out in the classes.

Overall, you might want to avoid obedience classes unless you are really struggling to teach your dog anything or your dog is engaging in negative behaviors.

If you do go to one of these classes then be sure you participate with the trainers so you can get the information you need on you to get your dog to listen to you among other points. Your dog will be more receptive to learn things if it is getting support from a familiar face and voice as well.

8) Adult Training

It is best to train your Jack Russell Terrier at an early age. However, this does not mean that it is too late to get the dog to learn something when it is older. Adult training can be used to make it easier for an older dog to learn new things.

Adult training is often used on dogs that have been found as strays. These include dogs that might not have gotten all that much human interaction early on in their lives.

This process is also done by many shelters and kennels that take care of such strays. They often work with certain processes before their dogs can be put up for adoption.

Still, you might want to see how to train an adult Jack yourself. There's never a true guarantee that a dog will actually listen to you right away.

There are several things for you to do when it comes to teaching your dog the right tricks at an older age.

1. First, make sure you have a good leash on hand.

2. Make sure you teach your dog to come first and foremost. You might have to gently pull on a chain while using a proper verbal command so the dog can associate your word with the action. Make sure you are very calm and gentle in the process of doing so.

3. Teach your dog to sit when you sit down yourself and you stop moving. Use this motion and a verbal command to get the older dog to notice that you are stopping and that the dog itself should do the same.

4. Push down on the dog's shoulders in a gentle manner to make it lie down. Let the dog gently feel this motion to give it the idea to sit down.

5. Make sure you give the dog a treat regardless of whether the dog follows a command on its own or you get the dog to do this by force. The dog will associate that pleasant thing with whatever you are trying to get it to do at a certain time.

6. Be sure to spend a few minutes each day teaching your adult dog these tricks. You must spend plenty of time to ensure that the dog will be more likely to listen to you and follow along with what you want out of it.

9) Stopping Distractions

Distractions can be bothersome to any dog. These distractions can range from an animal in an area to some person walking by. You have to be certain that you can keep your dog focused on you or other things you want that dog to do.

Naturally, it is no surprise that the dog can be as distracted as easily as it can. This comes from how the dog is known to be a good hunting dog. It might be on the lookout for things but that does not necessarily mean that it will be likely to stay focused on certain things as easily as you might wish it could.

The process of stopping such distractions from being any more of a hassle than they have to be is not too hard to follow along with though. There are many things that have to be done to keep distractions from being worse than they could be.

1. If the dog is distracted during a walk then increase the speed of your walk. This will get the dog to catch up with you and stay focused on the walk.

2. If the dog ever sees something in a yard then use a cue to get the dog to stop or come to you. In particular, have some treats out and use a particular command that you can use to tell the dog to stop. Place the treat in a spot that you want the dog to stop in so he or she will actually pay attention to your command. This might require a few attempts and trials but it can be done with care if you know what to get out of the process in some way.

3. Use a clicker or other item that emits a noise that your dog can link to you if it is distracted. Use that clicker and then add a word or other thing attached to it so the dog will become used to the command without having to use the clicker or other additional noise as it comes along.

10) How Often Should You Train Your Dog?

You can train your Jack Russell Terrier as often as you want. However, it is best to train your Jack at the right times when you know that the dog will actually be responsive to you.

You should train your Jack Russell Terrier at times when it has already run around and exercised. It will not be agitated or distracted at this point.

Also, make sure you train it after it uses the bathroom. Allow it to relieve itself so it will actually have a chance to focus.

It might also help to train it after you feed it. This is to keep the distraction of hunger or thirst from being a threat.

11) Your Tone Of Voice

The tone of voice that you will be using should be reviewed carefully. Sometimes the inflections of your voice will be the key between either your dog listening to you or the dog just shutting down and feeling unhappy around you.

A good thing to do with regards to the tone of your voice is to keep it consistent. You have to make sure you have a good tone that your dog will identify as being unique to you.

Your tone must also be upbeat and positive. Be sure that you sound happy to be around your dog and the dog will notice that you are being very careful around it.

Don't ever yell or get upset with your dog in any way. It is very easy for a dog to become fearful of someone who is loud or hostile in tone. Your Jack Russell Terrier will especially be vulnerable to problems that come from being overly loud.

You must make sure that your tone of voice is kept as comfortable as possible. Be easy with your words and associate them with positive tones and the right actions that the dog will understand.

If you are upbeat and providing the dog plenty of positive forms of stimuli then it should be easier for the dog to listen to you. You have to do this the right way to give your dog a positive idea of what you want to get out of it.

12) Handling Bad Habits

There are many bad habits that a dog can get over time. These are often caused by the dog's lack of understanding of certain things. In some cases they are caused by the dog just simply thinking that something is a toy.

However, in other cases these bad habits may be caused by the surroundings that a dog is in and by observing the behaviours of others.

These are problematic habits that any dog, including a Jack Russell Terrier, can easily get into. However, this does not mean that these problems have to persist forever. There are many ways how you can control some commonplace bad habits that your dog might get into.

Excess Barking

Excess barking is a common problem among many dogs with the Jack Russell Terrier being one that can especially engage in this activity.

However you can control problems relating to excess barking by using a few sensible steps to keep the dog comfortable and relaxed.

1. Gradually expose the dog to things that cause it to bark. Try to keep the dog nearby to show that there is no reason for the dog to become fearful of whatever it might see.

2. Interrupt the dog when it barks by using a "quiet" command. Be calm but steady when doing this. Reward the dog with something when the dog stops barking.

3. Use a stimuli that will come about with the distraction. Use something like a toy, treat or other item that keeps the dog from barking. Over time the dog will start to associate what was a distraction with a positive stimuli and will be less likely to bark at the wrong time.

Climbing on Furniture

If your dog climbs on the furniture in your home then you can use the following command ideas:

1. Tell the dog to get off. Use a gentle push with a command that will be linked to it.

2. Over time, see that the dog will respond to get off when you use the right command that is attached to the demand.

3. Be sure to reward the dog when it does get off. Make sure the treat is linked to the word you use to tell it to get off as well as the action of actually getting off.

Having a few pieces of furniture in the home for the dog to have many help as well. Dog furniture that is designed for the dog to lie on can always be found in a good variety of forms.

Chewing Things

From newspapers to clothes, it can be easy for a dog to chew things. Here are some steps to use to get a dog to stop chewing on those things:

1. Push on the dog's cheeks near the back of its jaw.
2. Praise the dog as it drops whatever it was holding.
3. Keep doing this as the dog chews something and it will begin to associate not chewing it with positive points.

This can be done as often as required but it should be easy for the dog to pick up on the fact that it should not be doing this in the first place.

As charming as your dog may look, you need to be careful with regards to how it acts. Make sure you watch for how it behaves and don't be afraid to correct your dog if needed.

Chapter 12: Medical Care and Safety

You need to be certain that your dog's medical safety is kept as a priority to you. There are many things that can be done to help keep your dog healthy.

Of course, your dog might become nervous over some medical-related things. However, if you are persistent and you understand what needs to be done when taking care of your dog then it will be easier for your friend to stay healthy.

The thing about the Jack Russell Terrier is that it is a dog that can live to be quite up there in age. If you understand what you are going to get out of your dog then it could be very easy for your dog to feel healthy.

In fact, if you use the right standards with regards to medical care then you will not only keep your dog healthy and happy but you will get to know more about your dog. You have to know quite a bit of things to ensure that your dog will feel happy; being with your dog throughout all of these medical inspections and reviews can make a difference.

1) Choosing a Veterinarian

A good veterinarian will help you out by taking a look at your Jack Russell Terrier on occasion and making sure that it is being taken care of as necessary. However, you might be surprised at the number of veterinarians that might be available to help take care of your Jack Russell Terrier.

There are several things to think about when it comes to checking on different veterinarians to see which ones might be right for the needs that your Jack Russell Terrier might have:

- See what types of pets your vet will specialize in. You might find some vets that can work with specific breeds like the Jack Russell Terrier above others.

- Ask about the experience that the vet has with breeds like yours.

- See what degrees the vet has. A good vet needs to be fully licensed.

- Look to see what services are available at a vet's office. These include not only regular services but also any emergency services that might be required. See if you can tell when you should and shouldn't get in touch with the doctor.

- See if the doctor you are visiting takes part in continuing education courses as a means of learning the newest trends and standards in animal care.

- Make sure your Jack Russell Terrier has a good sense of rapport with a vet of interest. This can make it easier for the dog to be taken care of the right way without any arguments in the process of doing so.

- See if the vet has been disciplined for any reason. Look into the reason as to why this professional has been punished as well.

Be careful when finding a good vet. You need to be certain that the vet you do get in touch with is capable of giving you the help that your dog deserves. More importantly, you need to be certain that your vet is one that you can be comfortable around.

2) Neutering and Spaying

A key aspect of care will entail spaying or neutering your Jack Russell Terrier.

Spaying refers to removing the reproductive features of the female while neutering is the same for the male. These processes are done as a means of keeping these dogs from reproducing, thus controlling the pet population in a safe manner.

The process works in a similar manner for either a male or female:

1. The pet is treated with an appropriate drug that will be used to sedate the animal. The pet will be under during the whole process.

2. An incision will then be made in a spot around the reproductive organs.

3. The doctor will then remove the necessary materials around the dog's region. The male's testes or the female's uterus will be removed at this point.

4. Dissolvable stitches are then used to seal off the site where the incision was made.

5. The pet will be kept for observation for a period of time. Sometimes the pet may be observed for a day. This is done to ensure that the pet will not touch or interfere with the incision site. This is also to ensure that there are no complications from the process and that the pet can fully recover after having been treated with such a procedure.

This is a process that should be done before the puppy reaches six months of age. It does not take much for a puppy to become capable of producing a litter around this point.

There are many different behavioral changes that will come around as a result of the process. Fortunately, these are all positive points:

- Your Jack Russell Terrier will be less likely to engage in the act of marking its territory with its urine.

- The dog will not be at risk of roaming or trying to escape from a spot. This is because the dog will not be in heat and looking for a partner to engage in sexual actions with.

- The sexual urges that your dog might hold will be eliminated. This makes it easier for the dog to focus on other things like training.

- A dog that has been fixed will not be as likely to be aggressive. The dog will be calm to the point where it will not be at as much of a risk to attack or bite other people as it might normally be.

- Behaviors that relate to the dog's dominance of certain situations will be eliminated or at least lessened in intensity too. These include problems relating to excess barking. There are times when your Jack Russell Terrier might continue to bark often but these problems may not be as prevalent or severe as they used to be.

There are added physical benefits to see too:

- The risk of developing certain forms of cancer relating to the testes or uterus will be eliminated.

- The dog will not be at risk of developing potentially harmful bacteria in the area that was removed.

- The dog will not worry about extreme physical stress that might come from giving birth or impregnation either.

You may want to be aware of how the dog could potentially gain weight though. Sometimes the changes in the dog's body after it has been fixed can cause its metabolic rate and appetite to change. This might make it to where the dog can easily gain weight. This is not always going to be a problem but it helps to be aware of this anyway.

Regardless of what may happen with your dog, you need to take a careful look at how the spaying or neutering process is to be done. If you get your dog to go through this process then it should be easier for your dog to stay healthy and happy.

3) Vaccinations

Vaccinations are critical to the health of your Jack Russell Terrier. Vaccinations are often used to take care of many problems relating to the dog's health.

The idea of administering a shot isn't something people are all that happy about but it is a small sacrifice for health. Your Jack will certainly be healthy and comfortable if you just provide it with a good series of vaccinations.

You need to vaccinate a puppy for many reasons:

- It can prevent serious diseases like distemper, rabies and many others.

- It also ensure that no one will be at risk of harm around

your dog.

- Your dog will be less likely to suffer from pains around its body when vaccinated.

- Most importantly, there are some cases where you might be in legal trouble if your dog is not vaccinated. This can especially be the case if a dog accidentally bites someone.

What Is Prevented?

Vaccinations for your Jack Russell Terrier can help prevent the following:

- Canine parvovirus – a contagious condition that causes extreme weight loss

- Distemper – a condition that will cause respiratory and central nervous system failures

- Rabies – where the saliva of the animal can cause muscle pain, vomiting and mental disorientation

- Canine hepatitis – a liver infection that keeps the body from being able to handle toxins and other problems that get into it

When Should You Vaccinate?

The time to vaccinate your dog should be reviewed with more than enough care. It's true that the milk from the puppy's mother will provide it with antibodies to protect itself but this will not be enough.

It helps to get the puppy vaccinated starting at an age of about 6 to 8 weeks.

The vaccinations should then be 3 to 4 weeks apart.

The last vaccinations need to be added at 16 weeks.

Naturally, there are times when you might find a Jack Russell Terrier puppy on the market that has received all its vaccinations. You need to talk with your provider to see if it has all the information on the vaccinations that it has received. This is to ensure that you will actually have a dog that has gotten the vaccinations that it does need.

Booster vaccinations may also be used. These are vaccinations that entail the dog receiving added support to prevent certain conditions from developing in its body.

Specifically, you need to ensure that your dog gets annual rabies vaccinations. These annual treatments are used to ensure that the dog will be fully covered against problems that may develop from rabies. This is used to keep a dog's coverage under control, what with rabies being a deadly condition that does not have a cure attached to it.

Are Vaccinations Safe?

Many people are often worried about whether or not vaccinations are safe. You might be surprised as to how many people say they don't want to get their dogs vaccinated.

However, these vaccines are designed to contain only the antibodies that the dog needs in order to fight off certain conditions. These are prepared without the use of many dangerous chemicals and are consistently being studied with the purpose of making them even more effective.

Don't ever feel as though choosing not to vaccinate your dog is a good idea. The odds are your dog will actually be at risk of serious harm if it is actually vaccinated.

4) De-worming

De-worming is a process where the dog will be treated for parasites. These include worms that live in the intestines of a dog and can make it ill. The process works in that the dog is fed a particular medicine that will help to force out the worms that the dog has.

This can also work for heartworm. This is a condition where a parasite might potentially get in the dog's heart and will have to be treated as soon as possible.

This is done as a means of clearing out worms and other parasites that have gotten into the dog's body and can live off of the linings of the dog's intestine. These can cause damages to the dog that may end up being fatal.

You will need to get your dog de-wormed in the event that the dog is experiencing these problems in its body:

- Coughing
- A lack of energy
- Substantial fatigue after exercising; that is, the dog will engage in the same amount of exercise it always gets but will feel even more fatigued
- A swollen belly; this may be due to fluid building up in the region due to the parasite's presence
- A decreased appetite; this can result in weight loss

As harmful as the condition can be, it can be treated if you get your dog out to a veterinarian. You must have the dog visit your vet to get the condition looked at and then treated properly.

The de-worming process works with the following steps:

1. A proper medication will have to be given to the dog. This often comes in the form of a special pill that should be easy for the dog to consume and digest.

There are some cases where a medication has to be injected into a particular spot in the body. This is especially the case for if the dog has heartworm.

2. The components in the medication will move into the intestinal tract or the heart depending on the treatment being used.

3. The exterior parts of the worms will be destroyed by the medication. This will cause the worms to weaken and die off.

4. The worms will eventually be removed from the body through the dog's fecal matter.

You must be careful with de-worming though. The medication that is to be used must be administered exactly as directed.

Also, if your dog has to take an injection-based medication for heartworm then there is a potential for the dog to need to be kept overnight for observation. This is due to some of the side effects that can come about from such a medication. The dog will have to be observed carefully to ensure that nothing wrong will come about within its body after the treatment is over.

In addition, your dog might have to receive a follow-up visit later on. This is to ensure that the condition is gone. A second oral medication may be used to clear out any larvae that the worms might have left in your dog's body. This in turn reduces the potential for more worms to come along.

Remember that this is a very important procedure that needs to be done as soon as possible. If your dog is not de-wormed then it may be at risk of harm with some cases resulting in death.

5) Tail Docking

Tail docking is a practice that is used on a puppy to remove its tail or at least a sizable portion of its tail. However, it is a practice that may not be recommended for a Jack Russell Terrier, what with its tail not being all that long. In fact, there is a potential that it may not be legal where you are.

This is a practice that works with a few steps in mind:

Surgical

Surgical scissors may be used as a means of removing the tail. A scalpel may also be used in some cases. The tail will be removed at the dock, the spot on the body where the tail connects to the rump.

Non-Surgical

A puppy's tail will be adjusted with a binding material on the outside near the dock. This will cause the blood flow to the tail to die off, thus making it easier for the tail to break off over time. This takes a few days or even weeks to complete and is typically done at a very early age when the dog will be less likely to fight back.

In particular, the dog will typically be about seven to fourteen days in age when this is done. This is around the time when the dog is small enough to have this done without the need to use any pain-killing medications.

Why Is This Done?

The practice of tail docking is used as a means of doing many things. It is believed to help with:

- Strengthening the dog's back

- Increasing its speed

- Keeping it from being at risk of certain injuries

- As a means of making the dog a little more focused in the hunting fields

- For show purposes

The reasons that people have for docking the tails of their dogs will vary but it's a practice that has been around for a long period of time. It fact, this is a practice that was done in the UK well before the nineteenth century as a means of getting dog owners to avoid taxes that were imposed on working dogs. This practice continues to be used in spite of this tax loophole being closed up all the way back in 1796.

Is This Legal?

The act of tail docking is legal in some spots but not all places will approve of it. In particular, it is a practice that anyone in North America can do. Meanwhile, it can be done in the UK provided that a vet takes care of it.

There are a few countries that have outlawed the act of tail docking. It is completely illegal in most parts of the European Union, particularly Ireland and Germany, and it is also illegal in Australia.

Overall, tail docking is not necessarily a required thing to do in all cases. It will not harm the dog in any manner but it is not like it is going to make a real difference. Whether or not your dog should have its tail docked should be determined upon your own particular discretion.

6) Ear Cropping

Ear cropping is another practice that many dog owners will engage in. This is especially the case for a dog like the Jack Russell Terrier. Its large ears can be trimmed down in size. However, it is not a process that is legal in all parts of the world.

Ear cropping works in that the outside flaps of the ears are removed. It is typically done in the same manner as that of the tail docking process in that it can be a surgical routine or a non-surgical procedure that has to be done as the puppy is very young.

Why Do People Do It?

People will crop the ears of their dogs for many reasons:

- It makes it easier for the inside parts of the ears to stay healthy. That is, they will not be at risk of developing harmful bacteria or other items that can harm the ears.

- Some people do this as a means of creating signifying features that show that a dog is the property of someone in particular.

- It may even be done to get a dog to meet certain breed standards at dog shows.

- The ears are even cropped because they might be seen as early targets for prey. That is, someone can grab at a dog's ears and drag it around, potentially causing even more harm.

Is It Legal?

There has been a great amount of debate over time as to whether or not cropping is a suitable practice for dog owners to use. This comes from people arguing that the practice is inhumane and that it does nothing for the benefit of the dog.

In fact, the practice is illegal in a number of places around the world. Specifically, it is banned in England, Scotland, France, Australia and Poland among other countries.

It is still legal in many parts of the United States and Canada. A few states have tried to pass bills that would make ear cropping illegal.

Also, not all parts of Canada have outlawed the act of cropping. It is officially outlawed in Manitoba and most of the Maritime provinces, particularly Nova Scotia and New Brunswick. However, it is legal in many other spots around the country.

Overall, ear cropping can be dangerous the dog. It is best to avoid this practice as it is not going to do much for your dog. In addition, it might be illegal where you are or could possibly become illegal at some point in the future.

7) Special Care When Pregnant

There is a potential for a female Jack to become pregnant. If she has not been spayed then she could get in heat and end up mating with a male, thus becoming pregnant.

You should not be afraid if you have a pregnant Jack. The fact is that you will have the opportunity to help her make it through a pregnancy so she can be healthy and capable of producing a healthy litter. You may even have some of these puppies on your own or you can at least offer them to others on the market for your own profit.

Still, it is critical to be certain that you are cautious when taking care of a pregnant dog. You must make sure that you take good care of your Jack Russell Terrier if it is pregnant. If you have a female then you need to be aware of how well she is responding if pregnant.

How To Tell She Is Pregnant

You can find out that your female is pregnant by visually looking at her body. It is often easy to see that she's pregnant after a few weeks but you need to be aware of the key signs that can come with your dog if she is pregnant. If you can identify these points as soon as possible then it will be easier to take care of her.

You can tell that a female is pregnant if she is:

- A little more withdrawn than usual

- Showing obviously nipple color changes

- Having a filled-out belly

- Is not eating as much as usual

You may want to talk with a vet to see if your Jack is pregnant. It helps to especially get her checked soon as a Jack can give birth about eight to nine weeks after becoming pregnant.

Points For Care

It is critical to ensure that you are careful when you dog is pregnant. You must be certain that you make her as comfortable as possible so the birthing process can go through without a hitch.

- Make sure the pregnant dog has plenty of rest so she will feel comfortable.

- Keep her from being in contact with other dogs. Be sure to especially keep her from males.

- Use a cardboard box with old newspapers as a good habitat for her to sleep in. This can help in the birthing process as she will be in a safe spot that is soft and comfortable.

- Add a bit of cottage cheese to your dog's diet. Only a small teaspoon is good enough. This will give her the calcium she needs while nursing.

- Don't let her jump for any purpose.

- Take care of the grooming process for her twice a week to ensure that she doesn't have any fleas or other things in her body.

- Check with your veterinarian to see if there are any 24-hour places that you can bring your dog to in the event that there are any problems with your dog. This is a time when the dog might become exceptionally vulnerable to certain physical problems. This can also be important if the dog is struggling during the birthing process.

Most of all have your pregnant Jack visit your veterinarian on occasion. Your vet should provide you with many great points on how to take care of the dog and also ensure that the dog is not at risk of serious complications.

Don't forget to make sure your newborn puppies are taken good care of as this happens. Your puppies need to be healthy and with their mother as they begin their lives.

Chapter 13: Micro-Chipping, Insurance and the Law

This chapter is all about the many legal considerations that come with having a Jack Russell Terrier. As great as it can be to have a dog like this, you need to be certain that you are watching for whatever may go along with your dog.

If you are unable to follow the standards here then you might be at risk of serious losses and legal trouble. There's also that potential that your dog could become lost.

1) Micro-Chipping

Micro-chipping is a practice that can be critical to your dog's health. Micro-chipping is a practice where a small identifying material is implanted under the dog's skin. This is a very small material that uses RFID, or radio frequency identification, technology to give off signals as to what the identity of a dog might be.

This is a safe and easy to use material. It is also designed to be fully supportive with the right components that will not wear out.

This is injected into the dog's body with a small syringe. This ID is unique and will list information on the dog's name, location and contact information on the owner. This is all done as a means of ensuring that the dog will be retrieved in the event that it is lost.

The legality of the micro-chipping practice is not totally universal just yet but it is a practice that has been used in a variety of places:

- It is not mandatory in the United States or Canada but it is strongly recommended. It can be offered by a vet for $25/£16 at its lowest cost.

- The practice is mandatory in Northern Ireland.

- The process will also be mandatory in England starting in 2016.

- It is also required in Japan, New Zealand and some parts of Australia (particularly New South Wales).

This chip can be quickly scanned with the use of a simple handheld device that can be used by the right authorities. A typical scanner can easily work on any dog that has such an implant.

2) Pet Insurance

Insurance is a very popular investment for all to have. If you are properly insured in any manner than you will be fully or at least mostly covered against many expenses that might come out of nowhere.

Auto, life and home insurance are always great to think about. However, you might want to consider pet insurance for your Jack Russell Terrier.

Pet insurance can be important to consider. This is a service that will cover the expenses that come with taking your dog to the vet and getting different medical services handled.

Pet insurance can be critical for cases where your Jack ends up suffering from serious physical problems or requires some kind of surgical procedure. Some problems that a dog can get into can cost thousands to resolve. Pet insurance can cover all the expenses that come with certain things that the dog might suffer from.

You are not required to get pet insurance but it might help for you to take a careful look at. This can really be crucial if your dog is at risk of certain medical conditions or comes from a line where certain problems might come about.

Be aware though that it can cost a good amount of money to get pet insurance. The total cost of your insurance can vary depending on where you go and on the medical points that relate to your pet. You might have to spend $50/£33 to get your dog insured each month, for instance.

Still, you can be reimbursed by 80% or more of the total cost of certain treatments that your dog requires. This is an important point to see as it proves that there is a real potential for you to keep your dog protected against serious threats that it might get into it.

Always check with any insurance provider to see what you can get out of a policy. All insurance companies have their own standards for what can be used to take care of the dog.

3) Licensing

Licensing is a good practice that can be critical for when you are trying to have a Jack Russell Terrier in your life. Licensing is needed to ensure that there is a record of you owning a dog.

This does not mean the dog needs to hold a license like you have. Rather, it is just to state that you are the owner of a particular dog and that you are liable for whatever the dog gets into. It is fun to consider just what a license for a dog would look like though.

There are several big reasons why licensing is so important to consider:

- It helps people to be aware of how your dog's vaccination schedule is going. This includes showing that your dog is up to date on vaccinations.

- There's a potential that you might be fined if your dog doesn't have a license. This is especially important if you will be traveling often with your dog or you are going to move to some new space with your dog.

- It will be much easier for your dog to be returned to you in the event that it ever goes missing.

Most importantly, having a license may be interpreted as mandatory in some parts of the world:

- Most parts of the United States require licenses.

- All major cities within Canada require dogs to be licensed. The standards will vary in different rural spots around the country.

- Licenses are required in both Northern Ireland and Ireland itself.
- Dogs in Australia and New Zealand also require their own licenses that will be registered by their local city or district councils.

Dogs in England do not have to be licensed; the standard for licensing in this part of the UK was eliminated back in 1987. Still, it might help to see if there is a potential for you to ask for proper identification features for your dog to use if you are going to have a Jack in that part of the UK.

Fortunately, it can only cost about $20/£13 to get a dog licensed each year. Be aware that this cost will be higher if the dog has not been spayed or neutered.

4) Legal Responsibilities

You must be very careful when it comes to having a dog. Even a normally safe dog like the Jack Russell Terrier can be dangerous if you are not careful. Here are a few of the key legal duties that you might have to bear with:

- You must be responsible for the protection of your dog and to ensure that it is kept in a safe space where it will not get in trouble with other people or cause some particular kind of harm in an area.
- You will be responsible for if your dog strays off and causes damage to someone's property.
- If a dog bites someone then there is a realistic potential that you could be at risk of being sued.
- If your pet injures another animal then you will be legally responsible for compensating the owner of the animal that your dog injured.

There are a few defenses that you could make though:

- In some cases damages that your dog causes can be due to someone provoking that dog into engaging in certain behaviors.

- Contributory negligence may occur in that you may be held liable for only part of the damages. This can come from another party not being careful around the dog and being irresponsible.

- The assumption of risk can occur in that someone might get in the way of a dog and will be at risk of serious problems because that someone has gotten into a condition that is clearly known to be unsafe and dangerous.

If you have any concerns about these legal points then talk with your lawyer or other local legal professional for help.

Chapter 14: Health Problems

Like with any other breed, the Jack Russell Terrier can develop certain health problems over time. You must be fully aware of the problems that your Jack Russell Terrier could potentially suffer from.

The problems that come with your dog's body can prove to be difficult to bear with. Still, these may be treated if you get in touch with a doctor for help as soon as possible. This is to see that you will get the problems that you have taken care of the right way without problems.

1) Signs Your Dog May Be Sick

Sometimes your dog might be sick and you don't even know it. There are a few things to watch for that can be telltale signs of illness in your Jack Russell Terrier:

- Excess urination or drinking
- Bad breath
- Substantial amounts of weight gain or loss
- Changes in the dog's appetite
- Difficulty in motion; this includes trouble with trying to climb up and down stairs
- Sleeping changes, most notable the dog sleeping for more time than usual
- Dry skin
- Constant itchiness
- Difficulties with breathing
- Potential spots or lumps that may be found around its skin
- Changes in the appearance of its eyes; they may become cloudy

If you can identify these problems as soon as possible and then have them taken care of then it should not be too hard for your dog to recover from certain problems. Remember, if your dog is struggling for too long then it will become sicker and harder to treat.

2) Common Health Concerns

There are many problems that a Jack Russell Terrier might develop that you need to be fully aware of. These are issues that have been known to be found in this breed quite often and deserve to be explored as needed.

Be aware that there is no guarantee that your Jack will actually suffer from these problems. This is just a listing of conditions that a Jack will be more susceptible of developing.

Lens Luxation

A lens luxation occurs when the lens in the eye dislocates. This can cause the dog to go blind. This is more likely to occur at an older age. In addition, this condition can cause pain and a reddish look in one's eyes.

Hernia

Jack Russell Terriers are more likely to suffer from hernias than other breeds. A hernia is a condition where an organ or tissue will move outward and create some bulge in the dog's body. A vet will have to perform surgery to fix this problem and keep it from becoming worse.

Hydrocephaly

Hydrocephaly occurs when the brain develops a high amount of fluid. This can cause the brain to suffer from pressure and therefore deteriorate quickly. The worst part of this condition is that it is untreatable.

This condition will typically be visible within a short period of time. This problem can cause an unusual appearance around the head that is untreatable. Sometimes a Jack or any other dog can live for a while after developing this condition but the overall timeframe for the dog's life will clearly vary on an individual basis.

Cryptochidism

Cryptochidism is a condition where the dog's testicles have not descended as well as they should. This can be a challenge for the spaying or neutering process.

Cardiomyopathy

A cardiomyopathy will occur when the heart's muscles start to become thick. This can cause the heart to struggle to work as it will become rather stiff in its tone.

This can be noticed by the dog breathing heavily. The worst part of this condition that occurs in many Jack Russell Terriers is that the dog's condition may not be all that easy to identify until after the dog has aged quite a bit.

Cerebellar Ataxia

A cerebellar ataxia is a condition that is inherited and can cause brain cells to die off. It can be noticed through changes in the dog's gait and times when the dog might start to walk into certain things. This is a condition that can progress at a varying rate; some dogs will end up degrading and wearing out quickly while others will bear with this condition over the course of years.

Take a look at your dog and see if it is walking with a gait that is rather stilted or otherwise off-beat in some manner. This is a sign of the condition. It gives off the appearance that the dog is not moving as well as it should.

Remember, you have to talk with your dog's breeder to see if there were ever any problems involving certain conditions in the dog's family line. You have to be aware of these problems if your dog's line appears to have them. It is true that many breeders are trying to eliminate these conditions as well as possible but it is important to understand what's important.

3) More Commonplace Concerns

There are some conditions that the Jack Russell Terrier can also suffer from. These are conditions that can occur among any dog breed and in some cases are conditions that your dog may not be genetically disposed to.

Here are a few of these issues:

Ear Infections

The long ears that the Jack Russell Terrier is known to hold can cause it to be at risk of ear infections. These can cause irritation in its ears and redness to go with it. In some cases these infections can cause the dog to develop deafness.

This is a point that will require the use of plenty of ear cleanings as mentioned earlier. You might also have to take your Jack Russell Terrier to a vet in the event that there is far too much stuff coming out of your dog's ears.

Obesity

Obesity is a concern that can develop in any dog but it can especially be prominent in the Jack Russell Terrier. This can occur if the dog is not active or you are feeding the dog far too much when compared with what it should really have.

The only real way to prevent this is to give your dog a healthy diet and ensure that it gets the exercise that it requires. Refer to the chapter on your dog's diet for added information on what needs to be done to keep your dog healthy and less likely to gain loads of weight.

High Toes

Having high toes is not a serious threat to the dog's life. However, it is a problem that can be an issue for some dogs. In fact, breeders are trying to get rid of this condition at this moment.

High toes occur when the dog's toes are short and do not appear to touch the ground. That is, the nails will appear to be hanging to where they will not touch the ground when walking. This is not going to be a serious problem for the dog over time but it is a condition that is not necessarily the most visually appealing.

Diabetes

Diabetes is not as commonplace in Jacks as they are in other dogs but it helps to be fully aware of this condition. Diabetes can be dangerous in that it can keep the dog from being able to handle sugars on its own. This can cause the dog to become overweight. In some cases you might have to use some insulin injections on your dog in the event that it suffers from diabetes.

In many cases dogs can develop diabetes if they are overweight. This comes from the added pressure that will come within the body from all the excess fats that it has developed.

4) When To Go To the Vet

If you ever see your Jack Russell Terrier struggling with its movements or behaving differently from usual then you need to take it to a vet as it could be suffering from one of these problems. Of course, there are no guarantees that any of these concerns that you have read about in this chapter will develop but it is important to know them as the Jack Russell Terrier will be more vulnerable to these issues than many other breeds in the world.

There are many times when it can be right for you to take your dog to a vet. Specifically, you should take the dog there if the dog is:

- Not eating as well as it should
- Constantly thirsty
- Vomiting regularly
- Experiencing substantial amounts of lethargy
- Has a stool that looks very unusual or odd
- Struggling to actually evacuate its bowels
- Experiencing sudden weight loss; a loss of about 10

percent of one's weight should be seen as a big problem

- Changes in one's eyes; this is especially the case if they start to appear cloudy or red

- Problems with its movements; these include cases where the rear is scooting or dragging

If you take your dog to a vet as soon as possible then it should not be too difficult for you to get your dog treated as needed. This is essential to see as some damages to your dog's body can prove to be very serious and threatening unless they are taken care of the right way.

5) Emergency Kit

A good emergency kit can be essential for when you are trying to take care of any serious problems that your dog might develop. Here are a few sensible things to have in your dog's emergency kit:

- Gauze pads

- Adhesive tape

- Saline; make sure it is fully sterile

- Hydrogen peroxide; this is to encourage vomiting

- A solution to treat cuts; rubbing alcohol is often useful in this case

- Tweezers

- Styptic pencil; this can help with keeping bleeding from being a problem, especially if you cut the dog's nails too low

- Antibiotic ointment

- Corn syrup; this is for a dog that is diabetic

- Cotton balls

- Antiseptic cleaning wipes

- Cloth strips; these are to keep the dog from biting a spot where something has happened on it

- Bandage that can cling to the dog's body

- A proper first aid book

- Phone numbers relating to who to contact in the event of an emergency involving your dog

You can often find a pet emergency kit at a typical pet supply store. If you do choose to go to a place like this then you must make sure that your kit has all of these components among other things.

6) Avoiding Health Problems

Obviously, the best way to avoid healthy problems is to see that your dog is in a line that is free from certain health conditions. Talking with a breeder about its overall health always helps.

However, there are often times when it might be difficult for you to actually find a dog that is free from such issues. You need to be aware of what you can do with your Jack Russell Terrier so you can understand what has to be done to keep your dog healthy.

Here are a few of the best things that you can do as a means of preventing certain health problems in your dog:

- Make sure your dog has plenty of fresh water for drinking. Be sure to replace the dog's water bowl every day.

- Give your dog plenty of healthy food; refer to the chapter about feeding in this guide for detailed information.

- Offer plenty of exercise; again, refer to the chapter in this book for information on making this work well.

- Always bring your dog to the vet each year for a full review. If you want to do this twice a year then you can do that as well.

- Always clean up after your dog when it uses the bathroom. Make sure you clean out all wastes that might be in a spot so the dog will not be hurt by any odors or other problems that might be found in one's wastes.

- Groom your dog as needed by brushing the coat, brushing its teeth and cleaning out its ears and eyes. Remember to review the grooming chapter of this guide for information on how to do this.

Be sure that you always watch for how your dog is behaving too. You need to be certain that your dog will be healthy for a long time but your own personal effort can be just as important.

7) Administering Medication

Medications are often used in cases where a dog is suffering from problems that require some kind of outside help. However, the practice of actually administering a medication can be tougher to handle than you might think.

Some dogs, particularly the Jack Russell Terrier, might be suspicious and may not be willing to take their medications. However, if you know what you have to do in the process of adding a medication then it should not be too hard to get a dog to want to take what it needs.

Only a veterinarian can prescribe medications to your Jack. Also, the veterinarian will more than likely not have a say as to how the medication is to be administered. This is due to many canine pharmaceutical companies only making medications that work with very specific administration standards in mind.

Pill

You will have to use this process to get a dog to take a pill or other oral-based medication:

1. Stick your thumb under a canine tooth and pressure upward on the roof of the dog's mouth.

2. Insert the pill deep to the back of the tongue as the mouth is open.

3. Close the mouth and then massage its throat until the dog

swallows.

There are times when you can actually get your dog's medication to mix in with its food. However, you need to talk with a vet about this before you can determine if it will be safe for you to put the medication in the dog's food.

Injection

For an injection-based medication, particularly one that is used for the treatment of diabetes, you will have to use the following steps to make it work:

1. Prepare a sterile needle for the injection; in most cases a medication like this will come with several needles that are disposable.

2. Target the appropriate space around the dog's body for the injection whether it is within a muscle or underneath the skin. Your doctor should tell you about where it will go.

3. Flick the syringe to get any bubbles to move up to the top of the unit so it will be easier to get the medication administered.

4. As the needle moves into the dog's body, make sure you watch how the medication moves into its body.

Be very cautious when using this kind of medication. In fact, you should only use this medication when the dog is calm and actually willing to take in the injection.

Liquid

Liquid-based medications are often easier for the body to absorb. Here are a few steps to use with liquid-based options in mind:

1. Prepare a plastic syringe, dropper or other item to load the medication in. Always use the required amount and nothing less or more. Some medications may even require you to mix their components before adding them.

2. Pinch the dog's lips and place the syringe or other item into the opening around the cheek.

3. Move the liquid into the dog's mouth. The dog should

swallow it not too long after you are done with this.

8) Buying Medications

You'll have to make sure you get the medications that your Jack requires on a regular basis. You'll need to keep plenty of medication on hand so your dog will not be at risk of harm from not being able to get the medications that it requires.

You can easily buy medications for your Jack Russell Terrier through one of many ways:

Through Your Vet

Your veterinarian will often provide you with direct access to any kind of medication that your dog needs. However, you need to watch for the price that comes with the treatment.

Some veterinarians will often charge more money for their medications. This is to ensure that the functions within an office can continue to operate as normal.

From a Pet Supply Store

Some major pet supply stores may have pet pharmacies on hand. These can provide you with proper dog medications provided that you have the medication certification and documents on hand.

You may receive a discount on your medications through a store like this. Be sure to check the values that such a place charges before committing to its services.

Online Stores

There are many popular online pet medication stores for you to choose from right now. These include places that promise to offer medications at discounts of up to half off of their standard values.

These places can offer discounts because the overhead charges associated with getting medications ready will be reduced. In addition, many of these medications will come directly from the companies that make them.

Still, you may want to see if a website that sells is medications will actually be reliable. You need to review the details on a website to see how it handles the shipments it gets and if it's safe to work with.

What Will Insurance Do?

Sometimes your insurance policy will cover the cost of the medications that you are trying to attain. However, there are often times when your policy is not going to protect you. For instance, it may not be available in the event that your dog's condition is deemed to be a pre-existing condition.

Also, an insurance policy may not be available if the dog is using any medication that hasn't been approved for sale by any appropriate governmental entity. Be sure to watch for this when finding out if your insurance will cover your dog's needs.

Chapter 15: Caring For an Aging Dog

As great as it can be to have a Jack Russell Terrier in your life, there is the obvious concern of what to do as it ages. You must make sure you care for your dog the right way as it gets up there in age.

Your senior dog will not be as active or energetic as it used to be. It may also be more susceptible to serious medical problems over time. It can also become more likely to be injured as the body is clearly not as strong as it used to be, thus creating a real concern for its condition after a while.

The worst part is that your dog might end up suffering to the point where it could be near death or even to where it has to be put down. This is never a good point to talk about but it is critical as it will be something to discuss over time.

1) Regular Care Points

There are a few points that need to be used when taking care of an aging dog. These relate heavily to how you are taking care of the dog as needed:

- Keep the diet for your dog as healthy as possible. Make sure you offer the best amounts of protein and nutrients possible. You might need to talk with your doctor about what can be used to keep your dog healthy.

It might help to provide your dog with plenty of fatty acids. These can help to improve the quality of the dog's joints.

- Make sure you give the dog the exercise that it wants. You might have to take shorter walks but be sure that you at least exercise the dog so it will be less likely to suffer from obesity or other weight-related problems.

- Always brush your dog's teeth on a regular basis. Older dogs are more likely to suffer from gingivitis and other dental-related concerns than younger dogs.

- Be observant of your dog's body. Look to see if it is developing lumps, losing weight or struggling with a weakened coat.

- See how your dog is moving as well. Watch to see if your dog is struggling with normal movements so you can see if you need to get your dog sent off to a vet for help.

Feeding

The feeding process should do more than just taking care of the dog's diet the right way. In addition to using more fatty acids to protect the dog's joints, you also need to keep the dog's caloric intake at a consistent rate.

It might help for you to feed your dog smaller meals at more frequent times during the day. This is to make it a little easier for the dog to consume the foods that it needs. This can be critical for a Jack Russell Terrier that needs hundreds of calories in a typical day.

Naturally, you might be recommended by your veterinarian to give your dog a diet that features foods that are formulated for an older dog's needs. These senior dog food products typically contain more fiber as a means of keeping digestive issues under control. The key at this point in the dog's life is to make sure the dog is actually digesting and consuming the foods that it is eating.

In addition, these high-fiber foods for seniors are made with fewer calories in mind. This should be good enough to protect the dog's health and to give it the energy that it requires in order to thrive.

Home Environment

The environment within your home needs to be checked as well:

- Keep a calm temperature within your home. Your Jack might become sensitive to extreme heat conditions.

- Try using ramps or other flat surfaces for a dog to move around on. Anything that keeps the dog from having to jump or move far too quickly will help.

- Keep your house clean so the dog will not be at risk of running into certain things. This is important as a Jack can be vulnerable to vision-related issues.

- Don't be too stressful around the dog. Make sure everything moves at a sensible pace and that you are not going to cause the dog to feel scared or surprised in any manner.

Your home should be seen as an inviting and comfortable place for the dog to live in. However, there are times when it might get to where there is nothing that can really be done for your dog.

2) When It's Time To Say Goodbye

It is not fair but the fact is that there can come a time when a dog is so ill and old that the best thing to do is to put it down. This can come from the dog's condition getting worse and the dog being in far too much pain.

As much as you may love your Jack Russell Terrier, you have to be aware of what you are doing with your dog in order to keep it treated right.

There are many times when you might know when it is time for you to say goodbye to your dog. You will need to seriously consider putting it to sleep if the dog is:

- Not enjoying the things that it used to like

- Extremely lethargic

- Suffering from a dramatic amount of weight loss

- Constantly vomiting

- Struggling to move due to pains around its body

- Refusing to respond to commands; in some cases the dog might not even hear or see them because it has become either deaf or blind

- Struggling to stay healthy in spite of having a decent diet

The best thing to do is to talk with your vet and to get your dog properly examined. In most cases the vet will find that there is some serious problem in the dog's body that has gotten to the point where it cannot be healed.

3) How Is the Pet Put Down?

The process of putting down a pet is by far the most difficult thing for a vet to do but it is often done with the welfare of that pet in mind. This is a process that will be used in the event that the dog's health is deteriorating.

Veterinarians will recommend this process when nothing else can be done for a dog. This is done as a means of keeping the dog from suffering from physical problems or stresses for far too long.

In addition, the process of putting the dog down is practically harmless. The dog will quickly be lulled into a sleep to where it can quickly die off. This is done without causing any more harm than what is needed.

There are many steps that are used in the process of putting down a dog or other pet:

1. The vet must get access to a proper vein in the dog's body.

2. The dog must be fully relaxed. You will have the option to be in the room with the dog at this point but this will be up to your own discretion.

3. An appropriate euthanasia solution will then be prepared. This is designed to help keep the dog's nerves from being active.

4. A medication or other material to keep the pet numb may also be used. This is to keep the pet from being agitated in any way as the solution is added into the vein.

5. If the needle is in the vein then the solution can be inserted into the vein.

6. In about ten seconds, the dog will breathe deeply and go to sleep.

7. The dog will be fully unconscious and will stop breathing

within a period of time.

8. The vet will then ask if you want to have some time alone with the pet's body. However, you can always choose to decline this if you are not all that comfortable.

9. The vet can then ask about the cremation process and if you want to keep the dog's ashes or if you want to have the dog buried.

This is obviously not the best experience to go through but it is an important one regardless. You need to make sure that the welfare of your dog is being taken care of if it is going to die soon. This process is simply used as a means of keeping the dog from suffering for far too long.

4) When Should You Get a New One?

The decision to have a new Jack or other dog in your life after your old dies can be a real challenge to bear with. Sure, you might miss the companionship that comes with having such a dog, but there is also the concern that you might be replacing the dog way too soon and may not be thinking about yourself.

You need to think about your grief and go through it to understand your connection with such a pet. While you might want to try and replace that old dog, the feelings that you have over that last dog may end up being pushed towards the new one. This can cause a strained relationship with your new dog.

If there are other people in your home then you need to talk with them about replacing the old pet. Everyone goes through the emotions of a loss on their own terms. You should avoid trying to replace a dog right away if people are uncomfortable.

You may also want to think about your responsibilities. Consider your lifestyle and living environment to see how it has changed over the years. There's always that potential that you might have to wait a bit before getting another dog.

If you do have another dog in the house or any other pet then you need to take that pet's welfare into consideration as well. Animals can grieve just as much as people can. With that in mind, you might want to consider how your dog is going to respond. Don't try to force a new dog into your current one's lifestyle or else that dog may not be all that happy.

The amount of time it will take between when you lose your old dog and when you should get your new one can be tough to figure out. Everyone responds to loss in their own ways. Be sure that you prepare yourself from a mental standpoint and consider your own needs when figuring out when you should have another dog.

Conclusion

If you have ever wanted to have a dog of your own then the Jack Russell Terrier will be a great dog for you to explore. This is a wonderful breed that is fun to have in your life but it is important to make sure you know how to take care of it so you can provide it with a long and happy life in a caring environment.

If you ever have an interest in buying a Jack Russell Terrier then you should know that you're making the right call. This is an amazing dog breed that has become a hit among people all around the world thanks to its many positive qualities.

The Jack Russell Terrier is a great dog with a good history to it that is reflective of the dog's natural ability to hunt. It has a beautiful and handsome look to it and will especially be happy to be around you.

Today the dog has become popular among pet owners thanks to how beautiful it is and how it has a great attitude. It does well when being trained and can get along with many people. Of course, you need to make sure the dog is treated properly and not placed in any danger so it will be comfortable around you and others in your home.

You must make sure that you take good care of your Jack Russell Terrier so it will be healthy as well. You have to use many standards to take good care of your dog's body by keeping your dog's diet and exercise routines healthy and happy.

The dog's health will start with you. You have to be careful with how you are feeding the dog while also observing the dog's condition as you take care of it. If you observe your dog's body then it should be very easy for the dog to feel comfortable and less likely to struggle with serious health-related issues over time.

Keeping a good environment for the dog can be important too. This includes not only having a good home for the dog but also a comfortable yard with plenty of outside space for the dog to roam all around in.

Having all the necessary materials that a dog requires in order to stay active can be just as important to think about. From assorted dog toys to the right pieces of grooming equipment, it will be important to give your dog all the love that you can give while also having the right materials for the job.

Speaking of which, don't forget to watch for how the dog is being treated from a grooming standpoint. Also, training can be easy to do if you just know how to make it work.

Have fun with your Jack Russell Terrier! You will certainly be happy with your dog as it will be there by your side for years to come.

Published by IMB Publishing 2015

Made in the USA
San Bernardino, CA
18 December 2017